WITH WORKBOOK

TOP NOTCH

English for Today's World

1B

WITH WORKBOOK

TOP NOTCH

English for Today's World

1B

Joan Saslow ■ Allen Ascher

With *Top Notch Pop Songs and Karaoke*
by Rob Morsberger

Top Notch: English for Today's World 1B with Workbook

Pearson Education, 10 Bank Street, White Plains, NY 10606

Editorial director: Pamela Fishman
Senior development editor: Peter Benson
Assistant development editor: Siobhan Sullivan
Vice president, director of design and production: Rhea Banker
Director of electronic production: Aliza Greenblatt
Managing editor: Mike Kemper
Production editor: Full-service production provided by Camelot Editorial Services
Art director: Ann France
Senior manufacturing buyer: Dave Dickey
Photo research: Aerin Csigay
Digital layout specialist: Warren Fischbach
Text composition: Studio Montage, Word & Image Design Studio, Inc.
Text font: Palatino 11/13, Frutiger 10/12

Photo credits: All original photography by Michal Heron. p. 69 (track) Tom Carter/PhotoEdit, (pool) Pat Lanza/Bruce Coleman Inc., (golf) David Cannon/Dorling Kindersley Media Library, (tennis) R.W. Jones/Corbis; pp. 69, 74 (park) Rudi Von Briel/PhotoEdit, (gym) David Sacks/Getty Images, (athletic field) Sergio Piumatti; p. 72 Martell/Boston Herald/Corbis Sygma; p. 76 (men's boxers, bathrobe) Comstock Royalty Free Division; pp. 76, 79 (windbreaker) Gerald Lopez/Dorling Kindersley Media Library, (handbag) Steve Gorton/Dorling Kindersley Media Library, (belt) Richard Megna, Fundamental Photographs, (running shoes) Siede Preis/Getty Images; p. 84 (top) Henry Herholdt/Getty Images, (middle) Wolfgang Kaehler Photography, (bottom) Fridmar Damm/eStock Photography LLC.; p. 88 (Rome) Louis A. Goldman/Photo Researchers, Inc., (Venice) Karen McCunnall/eStock Photography LLC, (Disney) Ron Dahlquist/SuperStock, (Magic Kingdom) Len Kaufman, (Africa) Gregory G. Dimijam MD/Photo Researchers, Inc.; p. 90 PhotoLibrary.com and Mark E. Gibson/Corbis; p. 92 Larry Williams/Corbis; p. 93 (zoo) Lawrence Migdale/Pix, (baseball game) SuperStock, (movie) Andre Jenny/ ImageState, (museum) Bob Krist/eStock Photography LLC.; p. 94 (Bhutan) Pete Oxford/Robert Harding World Imagery, (Rio) Stephanie Maze/Woodfin Camp & Associates, (students) Royalty Free/Corbis, (Sea Mountain) Rob Lewine/Corbis; p. 100 Gary Conner/Index Stock Imagery; p. 101 (station) Jeffrey Blackman/Index Stock Imagery, (train) Steve Vidler/eStock Photography LLC; p. 102 (Puebla) Chris Sharp/D. Donne Bryant Stock Photography; p. 104 Hans Georg Roth/Corbis; p. 106 Andres Morya Hinojosa/Morya Photography; p. 108 (train) Jim Winkley/Corbis, (ship) Ron Chapple/Getty Images; p. 114 (background) David Young-Wolff/PhotoEdit; p. 115 (digital camera) Epson America, Inc., (camcorder) Sony Electronics Inc., (DVD player) George B. Diebold/Corbis & Tom Carter/PhotoEdit, (MP3) William Whitehurst/Corbis, (scanner) Churchill & Klehr/Pearson Education/PH College; p. 121 Getty Images; p. W49 Richard T. Nowitz/Corbis; p. W54 Michal Heron; p. W59 Michal Heron; p. W60 (hair dryer) Silver Burdett Ginn, (photocopier) Getty Images; p. W61 (grandparents) Lindy Powers/Index Stock Imagery, (children; boots) Michal Heron; p. W64 (left) Jess Stock/Getty Images, (middle left) Dorling Kindersley Media Library, (middle right) Thomas Craig/Index Stock Imagery, (right) Robert Holmes/Corbis; p. W67 Ron Chapple/Getty Images; p. W69 Phil Cantor/Index Stock Imagery; p. W71 Bill Bachmann/ Index Stock Imagery; p. W73 Royalty-Free/Corbis; (bottom) LWA-Dann Tardif/Corbis; (right) James Marshall/Corbis; p. W78 Steve Vidler/ eStock Photography LLC; p. W79 Michal Heron; p. W88 Michal Heron, (right) Courtesy of West Edmonton Mall.

Illustration credits: M. Teresa Aguilar, pp. 100, 103; Steve Attoe, pp. W58 (bottom), W76; Kenneth Batelman, pp. 80, 83, 88, 89, 102, 109, 110, 117 (middle), W60, W61, W64; Pierre Berthiaume, pp. 106, 110, W82; Rich Burlew, p. 64, W49; John Ceballos, pp. 87, 99, 111, 123; Lane DuPont, p. 82 (bottom); Leanne Franson, pp. W62, W68; Scott Fray, pp. W60, W61; Steve Gardner, p. 112; (bottom), W90; Marty Harris, p. 91 (middle); Brian Hughes, pp. 82 (top), 115, W87; André Labrie p. W72; Andy Meyer, pp. 107, 108 (top), W81, W82; Suzanne Mogensen, pp. W80, W85; Sandy Nichols, pp. 58, 65, 66, 69, 70, 94, 104, 108 110, 119; NSV Productions, pp. W58 (top), W86, W87; Dusan Petriçic, pp. 68, 96, 120, W60, W83; Michel Rabagliati, p. W63; Robert Saunders, pp. 90, 91 (top); Phil Scheuer, pp. 116, 117 (top).

ISBNs: 0-13-110414-4 (Student's Book with Workbook and Audio CD)
0-13-229320-X (Student's Book with Workbook and Take-Home Super CD-ROM)

Printed in the United States of America
5 6 7 8 9 10–QWD–10 09 08 07

Contents

Scope and Sequence for 1A and 1B

UNIT	Vocabulary*	Conversation Strategies	Grammar	GRAMMAR BOOSTER
1 Getting Acquainted *Page 4*	• Titles • Occupations • Nationalities	• Use As a matter of fact to introduce surprising information • Begin responses with a question to clarify • Provide information beyond Yes or No when answering a question	• The verb be: Yes / no questions Contractions Information questions • Possessive nouns and adjectives	• Further explanation of usage and form: be • Further explanation of form: possessive adjectives
2 Going Out *Page 16* *Top Notch* Song: "Going Out"	• Entertainment events • Kinds of music • Locations and directions	• Use Really? to show enthusiasm • Use I'd love to to accept an invitation • Use I'd love to, but... or Thanks, but... to decline • Use Excuse me to approach a stranger	• The verb be: Questions with When, What time, and Where Contractions • Prepositions of time and place: On, in, at	• Further explanation of usage: prepositions of time and place
3 Talking about Families *Page 28*	• Family relationships • Ways to describe similarities and differences • Marital status and relationships	• Start answers with Well to give oneself time to think • Use That's great! to show enthusiasm • Ask follow-up questions to keep a conversation going • Initiate polite conversation with So	• The simple present tense: Statements Yes / no questions Information questions	• Further explanation of usage and form: the simple present tense
4 Coping with Technology *Page 40*	• Descriptive adjectives • Electronics • Ways to sympathize • Machines at home and at work • Machine features • Ways to state a complaint	• Use How's it going? and Hey to greet someone informally • Use word stress to clarify meaning • Use What about...? to make a suggestion • Use Really? to ask for confirmation • Use Hello? to answer the telephone	• The present continuous: for actions in progress and the future	• Spelling rules for the present participle • Further explanation of form: the present continuous
5 Eating in, Eating out *Page 52* *Top Notch* Song: "The World Café"	• Menu items • Categories of food • What to say to a waiter or waitress • Food and health	• Use I think I'll have to soften food orders • Use Good idea! to accept a suggestion enthusiastically	• Count and non-count nouns / there is and there are • A, an, the	• Categories of non-count nouns • Verb agreement: non-count nouns • Expressing quantities: non-count nouns • How much / How many • Spelling rules: plural nouns • Some / any

*In *Top Notch*, the term *vocabulary* refers to individual words, phrases, and expressions.

Speaking	Pronunciation	Listening	Reading	Writing
• Exchange personal information • Clarify and confirm information • Offer to introduce someone • Introduce someone • Shift to informality	• Rising and falling intonation for questions	• Conversations about people Task: listen for names, occupations, and nationalities	• Short introductions to people who travel for their jobs • Student descriptions	• Introduce a classmate • Introduce yourself
• Offer, accept, and decline invitations • Ask and answer questions about events • Ask for and give directions • Talk about music likes and dislikes	• Repetition to confirm information	• Invitations to events Task: identify the events and times • Phone calls to a box office Task: identify events, times, and ticket prices	• Newspaper entertainment listings • Arts festival website • People's descriptions of their musical tastes • Music survey	• Describe your own musical tastes
• Identify family relationships • Ask about and describe family members • Compare people • Discuss family size	• Blending sounds: Does + he / Does + she	• Descriptions of family members Task: listen for people's marital status or relationship • An interview about a brother Task: determine similarities and differences • Descriptions of families Task: determine size of family and number of children	• Article about different family sizes • Article comparing a brother and sister	• Compare two people in your own family • Compare two siblings in another family
• Ask for and make suggestions • Offer reasons for purchasing a product • Express frustration and offer sympathy • Describe features of machines • Complain when things don't work	• Rising and falling intonation for questions: review	• Complaints about machines Task: identify the machines • Radio advertisements Task: listen for adjectives that describe machines • Complaints to a hotel front desk Task: identify the problem and room number • Problems with machines Task: write the problem	• Ads from electronics catalogs	• Describe one of your own machines • Describe all the problems in a picture
• Discuss what to eat • Order, get the check, and pay for a meal • Describe your own diet • Discuss food and health choices	• Pronunciation of the before consonant and vowel sounds	• Conversations about food Task: listen for and classify food items • Conversations in a restaurant Task: predict a diner's next statement • Conversations while eating Task: determine the location of the conversation	• Menus • Nutrition website	• Describe a traditional food in your own country • Write a story based on a picture

Scope and Sequence for 1A and 1B

UNIT	Vocabulary	Conversation Strategies	Grammar	GRAMMAR BOOSTER
6 **Staying in Shape** *Page 64* *Top Notch* Song: "A Typical Day"	• Physical and everyday activities • Places for sports and games • Talking about health habits	• Use Sorry, I can't to decline regretfully • Provide an explanation for declining an invitation • Use Actually to introduce contrast	• Can and have to • The simple present tense and the present continuous • Frequency adverbs • Time expressions	• Further explanation of form: can / have to • Non-action verbs • Further explanation of usage and form: frequency adverbs / time expressions
7 **Finding Something to Wear** *Page 76*	• Categories of clothing • Clothing described as "pairs" • Types of clothing and shoes • Interior locations and directions • Describing clothes	• Use Excuse me to indicate that you need assistance in a store • Use Excuse me? when you don't understand or didn't hear	• Comparative adjectives • Object pronouns: as direct objects and in prepositional phrases	• Further explanation of spelling and usage: comparative adjectives • Further explanation of usage: direct and indirect objects
8 **Getting Away** *Page 88* *Top Notch* Song: "My Dream Vacation"	• Types of vacations • Adjectives for travel conditions • Adjectives to describe vacations • Travel problems	• Use actually to acknowledge another's interest • Say I'm fine to decline assistance • After answering a question, ask What about you? to show reciprocal interest	• The past tense of be • The simple past tense: regular and irregular verbs	• Further explanation of usage and form: the past tense of be • Further explanation of usage and form: the simple past tense • Spelling rules: regular verbs in the simple past tense
9 **Taking Transportation** *Page 100*	• Tickets and trips • Travel services • Airline passenger information • Means of transportation • Transportation problems	• Say Oh no to indicate dismay • Say Let me check to buy time to find the answer to a question	• Could and should • Be going to for the future	• Further explanation of meaning: can, should, could • Explanation of form: modals • Comparison of ways to express the future
10 **Shopping Smart** *Page 112* *Top Notch* Song: "Shopping for Souvenirs"	• Money and travel • Electronic products • Handicrafts • Talking about prices	• Use can to indicate willingness to bargain • Use demonstratives to clarify intention	• Superlative adjectives • Too and enough	• Contrasting the comparative and the superlative • Spelling rules for superlatives • Intensifiers too, really, and very

Speaking	Pronunciation	Listening	Reading	Writing
• Suggest and plan an activity • Provide an excuse • Ask about and describe daily routines • Discuss exercise and diet	• Can / can't • Third-person singular endings	• Conversations about immediate plans Task: identify destinations • Descriptions of exercise and diet routines Task: identify each person's health habits • Conversations about diet and exercise Task: complete the statement	• Graph showing calories burned by activity • Health survey • Article about Brooke Ellison's daily schedule	• Report about a classmate's typical day • Recount your own typical day
• Discuss where you shop • Ask a clerk for help • Shop and pay for clothes • Ask for and give directions within a building • Discuss culturally appropriate dress	• Contrastive stress for clarification	• Conversations about clothing needs Task: choose the clothing item • Directions in a store Task: mark the store departments • Conversations about clothes Task: determine the location of the conversation	• Clothing store website • Article about clothing tips for travelers • Personal dress code survey	• Give advice about clothing for visitors to your country • Plan clothing for a trip and explain reasons
• Greet someone arriving from a trip • Describe travel conditions • Talk about leisure activities • Discuss vacation preferences • Complain about travel problems	• Simple past-tense endings	• Descriptions of vacations Task: identify the vacation problems • Descriptions of travel experiences Task: choose the correct adjective	• Vacation ads • Travel agency brochure • Vacation survey • Student articles about vacations	• Describe a past vacation • Describe another person's vacation
• Discuss schedules and buy tickets • Ask for and give advice • Book travel services • Discuss travel plans • Describe transportation problems	• Intonation of alternatives	• Requests for travel services Task: identify the service requested • Airport announcements Task: listen for delays and cancellations • Conversations about transportation problems Task: complete the statement • Conversations about transportation Task: match the conversation with the picture	• Airport departure schedule • Travel survey • News clippings about transportation problems	• Recount transportation problems on a past trip • Imagine your next trip
• Ask for and give a recommendation • Discuss price range • Bargain for a lower price • Discuss tipping customs • Describe a shopping experience	• Rising intonation to clarify information	• Recommendations for electronic products Task: identify the product • Shopping stories Task: listen for products and prices • Conversations about electronics purchases Task: check satisfactory or not satisfactory to the customer	• Travel guide about money and shopping • Article about tipping customs • Tipping survey • Story about a shopping experience	• Narrate a true story about a shopping experience • Create a shopping guide for your city

Acknowledgments

Top Notch International Advisory Board

The authors gratefully acknowledge the substantive and formative contributions of the members of the International Advisory Board.

CHERYL BELL, Middlesex County College, Middlesex, New Jersey, USA • **ELMA CABAHUG**, City College of San Francisco, San Francisco, California, USA • **JO CARAGATA**, Mukogawa Women's University, Hyogo, Japan • **ANN CARTIER**, Palo Alto Adult School, Palo Alto, California, USA • **TERRENCE FELLNER**, Himeji Dokkyo University, Hyogo, Japan • **JOHN FUJIMORI**, Meiji Gakuin High School, Tokyo, Japan • **ARETA ULHANA GALAT**, Escola Superior de Estudos Empresariais e Informática, Curitiba, Brazil • **DOREEN M. GAYLORD**, Kanazawa Technical College, Ishikawa, Japan • **EMILY GEHRMAN**, Newton International College, Garden Grove, California, USA • **ANN-MARIE HADZIMA**, National Taiwan University, Taipei, Taiwan • **KAREN KYONG-AI PARK**, Seoul National University, Seoul, Korea • **ANA PATRICIA MARTÍNEZ VITE DIP. R.S.A.**, Universidad del Valle de México, Mexico City, Mexico • **MICHELLE ANN MERRITT, PROULEX/** Universidad de Guadalajara, Guadalajara, Mexico • **ADRIANNE P. OCHOA**, Georgia State University, Atlanta, Georgia, USA • **LOUIS PARDILLO**, Korea Herald English Institute, Seoul, Korea • **THELMA PERES**, Casa Thomas Jefferson, Brasilia, Brazil • **DIANNE RUGGIERO**, Broward Community College, Davie, Florida, USA • **KEN SCHMIDT**, Tohoku Fukushi University, Sendai, Japan • **ALISA A. TAKEUCHI**, Garden Grove Adult Education, Garden Grove, California, USA • **JOSEPHINE TAYLOR**, Centro Colombo Americano, Bogotá, Colombia • **PATRICIA VECIÑO**, Instituto Cultural Argentino Norteamericano, Buenos Aires, Argentina • **FRANCES WESTBROOK**, AUA Language Center, Bangkok, Thailand

Reviewers and Piloters

Many thanks also to the reviewers and piloters all over the world who reviewed *Top Notch* in its final form.

G. Julian Abaqueta, Huachiew Chalermprakiet University, Samutprakarn, Thailand • **David Aline**, Kanagawa University, Kanagawa, Japan • **Marcia Alves**, Centro Cultural Brasil Estados Unidos, Franca, Brazil • **Yousef Al-Yacoub**, Qatar Petroleum, Doha, Qatar • **Maristela Barbosa Silveira e Silva**, Instituto Cultural Brasil-Estados Unidos, Manaus, Brazil • **Beth Bartlett**, Centro Colombo Americano, Cali, Colombia • **Carla Battigelli**, University of Zulia, Maracaibo, Venezuela • **Claudia Bautista**, C.B.C., Caracas, Venezuela • **Rob Bell**, Shumei Yachiyo High School, Chiba, Japan • **Dr. Maher Ben Moussa**, Sharjah University, Sharjah, United Arab Emirates • **Elaine Cantor**, Englewood Senior High School, Jacksonville, Florida, USA • **María Aparecida Capellari, SENAC**, São Paulo, Brazil • **Eunice Carrillo Ramos**, Colegio Durango, Naucalpan, Mexico • **Janette Carvalhinho de Oliveira**, Centro de Linguas (UFES), Vitória, Brazil • **María Amelia Carvalho Fonseca**, Centro Cultural Brasil-Estados Unidos, Belém, Brazil • **Audy Castañeda**, Instituto Pedagógico de Caracas, Caracas, Venezuela • **Ching-Fen Chang**, National Chiao Tung University, Hsinchu, Taiwan • **Ying-Yu Chen**, Chinese Culture University, Taipei, Taiwan • **Joyce Chin**, The Language Training and Testing Center, Taipei, Taiwan • **Eun Cho**, Pagoda Language School, Seoul, Korea • **Hyungzung Cho**, MBC Language Institute, Seoul, Korea • **Dong Sua Choi**, MBC Language Institute, Seoul, Korea • **Jeong Mi Choi**, Freelancer, Seoul, Korea • **Peter Chun**, Pagoda Language School, Seoul, Korea • **Eduardo Corbo**, Legacy ELT, Salto, Uruguay • **Marie Cosgrove**, Surugadai University, Saitama, Japan • **María Antonieta Covarrubias Souza**, Centro Escolar Akela, Mexico City, Mexico • **Katy Cox**, Casa Thomas Jefferson, Brasilia, Brazil • **Michael Donovan**, Gakushuin University, Tokyo, Japan • **Stewart Dorward**, Shumei Eiko High School, Saitama, Japan • **Ney Eric Espina**, Centro Venezolano Americano del Zulia, Maracaibo, Venezuela • **Edith Espino**, Centro Especializado de Lenguas - Universidad Tecnológica de Panamá, El Dorado, Panama • **Allen P. Fermon**, Instituto Brasil-Estados Unidos, Ceará, Brazil • **Simão Ferreira Banha**, Phil Young's English School, Curitiba, Brazil • **María Elena Flores Lara**, Colegio Mercedes, Mexico City, Mexico • **Valesca Fróis Nassif**, Associação Cultural Brasil-Estados Unidos, Salvador, Brazil • **José Fuentes**, Empire Language Consulting, Caracas, Venezuela • **José Luis Guerrero**, Colegio Cristóbal Colón, Mexico City, Mexico • **Claudia Patricia Gutiérrez**, Centro Colombo Americano, Cali, Colombia • **Valerie Hansford**, Asia University, Tokyo, Japan • **Gene Hardstark**, Dotkyo University, Saitama, Japan • **Maiko Hata**, Kansai University, Osaka, Japan • **Susan Elizabeth Haydock Miranda de Araujo**, Centro Cultural Brasil Estados Unidos, Belém, Brazil • **Gabriela Herrera**, Fundametal, Valencia, Venezuela • **Sandy Ho**, GEOS International, New York, New York, USA • **Yuri Hosoda**, Showa Women's University, Tokyo, Japan • **Hsiao-I Hou**, Shu-Te University, Kaohsiung County, Taiwan • **Kuei-ping Hsu**, National Tsing Hua University, Hsinchu, Taiwan • **Chia-yu Huang**, National Tsing Hua University, Hsinchu, Taiwan • **Caroline C. Hwang**, National Taipei University of Science and Technology, Taipei, Taiwan • **Diana Jones**, Angloamericano, Mexico City, Mexico • **Eunjeong Kim**, Freelancer, Seoul, Korea • **Julian Charles King**, Qatar Petroleum, Doha, Qatar • **Bruce Lee**, CIE: Foreign Language Institute, Seoul, Korea • **Myunghee Lee**, MBC Language Institute, Seoul, Korea • **Naidnapa Leoprasertkul**, Language Development Center, Mahasarakham University, Mahasarakham, Thailand • **Eleanor S. Leu**, Souchow University, Taipei, Taiwan • **Eliza Liu**, Chinese Culture University, Taipei, Taiwan • **Carlos Lizárraga**, Angloamericano, Mexico City, Mexico • **Philippe Loussarevian**, Keio University Shonan Fujisawa High School, Kanagawa, Japan • **Jonathan Lynch**, Azabu University, Tokyo, Japan • **Thomas Mach**, Konan University, Hyogo, Japan • **Lilian Mandel Civatti**, Associação Cultural Brasil-Estados Unidos, Salvador, Brazil • **Hakan Mansuroglu**, Zoni Language Center, West New York, New Jersey, USA • **Martha McGaughey**, Language Training Institute, Englewood Cliffs, New Jersey, USA • **David Mendoza Plascencia**, Instituto Internacional de Idiomas, Naucalpan, Mexico • **Theresa Mezo**, Interamerican University, Río Piedras, Puerto Rico • **Luz Adriana Montenegro Silva**, Colegio CAFAM, Bogotá, Colombia • **Magali de Moraes Menti**, Instituto Lingua, Porto Alegre, Brazil • **Massoud Moslehpour**, The Overseas Chinese Institute of Technology, Taichung, Taiwan • **Jennifer Nam**, IKE, Seoul, Korea • **Marcos Norelle F. Victor**, Instituto Brasil-Estados Unidos, Ceará, Brazil • **Luz María Olvera**, Instituto Juventud del Estado de México, Naucalpan, Mexico • **Roxana Orrego Ramírez**, Universidad Diego Portales, Santiago, Chile • **Ming-Jong Pan**, National Central University, Jhongli City, Taiwan • **Sandy Park**, Topia Language School, Seoul, Korea • **Patrícia Elizabeth Peres Martins**, Instituto Brasil-Estados Unidos, Rio de Janeiro, Brazil • **Rodrigo Peza**, Passport Language Centers, Bogotá, Colombia • **William Porter**, Osaka Institute of Technology, Osaka, Japan • **Caleb Prichard**, Kwansei Gakuin University, Hyogo, Japan • **Mirna Quintero**, Instituto Pedagógico de Caracas, Caracas, Venezuela • **Roberto Rabbini**, Seigakuin University, Saitama, Japan • **Terri Rapoport**, Berkeley College, White Plains, New York, USA • **Yvette Rieser**, Centro Electrónico de Idiomas, Maracaibo, Venezuela • **Orlando Rodríguez**, New English Teaching School, Paysandu, Uruguay • **Mayra Rosario**, Pontificia Universidad Católica Madre y Maestra, Santiago, Dominican Republic • **Peter Scout**, Sakura no Seibo Junior College, Fukushima, Japan • **Jungyeon Shim**, EG School, Seoul, Korea • **Keum Ok Song**, MBC Language Institute, Seoul, Korea • **Assistant Professor Dr. Reongrudee Soonthornmanee**, Chulalongkorn University Language Institute, Bangkok, Thailand • **Claudia Stanisclause**, The Language College, Maracay, Venezuela • **Tom Suh**, The Princeton Review, Seoul, Korea • **Phiphawin Suphawat**, KhonKaen University, KhonKaen, Thailand • **Craig Sweet**, Poole Gakuin Junior and Senior High Schools, Osaka, Japan • **Yi-nien Josephine Twu**, National Tsing Hua University, Hsinchu, Taiwan • **Maria Christina Uchôa Close**, Instituto Cultural Brasil-Estados Unidos, São José dos Campos, Brazil • **Luz Vanegas Lopera**, Lexicom The Place For Learning English, Medellín, Colombia • **Julieta Vasconcelos García**, Centro Escolar del Lago, A.C., Mexico City, Mexico • **Carol Vaughan**, Kanto Kokusai High School, Tokyo, Japan • **Patricia Celia Veciño**, Instituto Cultural Argentino Norteamericano, Buenos Aires, Argentina • **Isabela Villas Boas**, Casa Thomas Jefferson, Brasilia, Brazil • **Iole Vitti**, Peanuts English School, Poços de Caldas, Brazil • **Gabi Witthaus**, Qatar Petroleum, Doha, Qatar • **Yi-Ling Wu**, Shih Chien University, Taipei, Taiwan • **Chad Wynne**, Osaka Keizai University, Osaka, Japan • **Belkis Yanes**, Freelance Instructor, Caracas, Venezuela • **I-Chieh Yang**, Chung-kuo Institute of Technology, Taipei, Taiwan • **Emil Ysona**, Instituto Cultural Dominico-Americano, Santo Domingo, Dominican Republic • **Chi-fang Yu**, Soo Chow University, Taipei, Taiwan, • **Shigeki Yusa**, Sendai Shirayuri Women's College, Sendai, Japan

To the Teacher

What is *Top Notch*?

- *Top Notch* is a six-level communicative English course for adults and young adults, with two beginning entry levels.
- *Top Notch* prepares students to interact successfully and confidently with both native and non-native speakers of English.
- *Top Notch* demonstrably brings students to a "Top Notch" level of communicative competence.

Key Elements of the *Top Notch* Instructional Design

Concise two-page lessons

Each easy-to-teach two-page lesson is designed for one class session and begins with a clearly stated communication goal and ends with controlled or free communication practice. Each lesson provides vocabulary, grammar, and social language contextualized in all four skills, keeping the pace of a class session lively and varied.

Daily confirmation of progress

Adult and young adult students need to observe and confirm their own progress. In *Top Notch*, students conclude each class session with a controlled or free practice activity that demonstrates their ability to use new vocabulary, grammar, and social language. This motivates and keeps students eager to continue their study of English and builds their pride in being able to speak accurately, fluently, and authentically.

Real language

Carefully exposing students to authentic, natural English, both receptively and productively, is a necessary component of building understanding and expression. All conversation models feature the language people really use; nowhere to be found is "textbook English" written merely to exemplify grammar.

Practical content

In addition to classic topical vocabulary, grammar, and conversation, *Top Notch* includes systematic practice of highly practical language, such as: how to ask for a restaurant check, how to ask whether the tip is included in the bill, how to complain when the air-conditioning in a hotel room doesn't work, how to bargain for a lower price—usable language today's students want and need.

Memorable model conversations

Effective language instruction must make language memorable. The full range of social and functional communicative needs is presented through practical model conversations that are intensively practiced and manipulated, first within a guided model and then in freer and more personalized formats.

High-impact vocabulary syllabus

In order to ensure students' solid acquisition of vocabulary essential for communication, *Top Notch* contains explicit presentation, practice, and systematic extended recycling of words, collocations, and expressions appropriate at each level of study. The extensive captioned illustrations, photos, definitions, examples, and contextualized sentences remove doubts about meaning and provide a permanent in-book reference for student test preparation. An added benefit is that teachers don't have to search for pictures to bring to class and don't have to resort to translating vocabulary into the students' native language.

Learner-supportive grammar

Grammar is approached explicitly and cognitively, through form, meaning, and use—both within the Student's Book units and in a bound-in Grammar Booster. Charts provide examples and paradigms enhanced by simple usage notes at students' level of comprehension. This takes the guesswork out of meaning, makes lesson preparation easier for teachers, and provides students with comprehensible charts for permanent reference and test preparation. All presentations of grammar are followed by exercises to ensure adequate practice.

English as an international language

Top Notch prepares students for interaction with both native and non-native speakers of English, both linguistically and culturally. English is treated as an international language, rather than the language of a particular country or region. In addition, *Top Notch* helps students develop a cultural fluency by creating an awareness of the varied rules across cultures for: politeness, greetings and introductions, appropriateness of dress in different settings, conversation do's and taboos, table manners, and other similar issues.

Two beginning-level texts

Beginning students can be placed either in *Top Notch 1* or *Top Notch Fundamentals*, depending on ability and background. Even absolute beginners can start with confidence in *Top Notch* Fundamentals. False beginners can begin with *Top Notch 1*. The *Top Notch Placement Test* clarifies the best placement within the series.

Estimated teaching time

Each level of *Top Notch* is designed for 60 to 90 instructional hours and contains a full range of supplementary components and enrichment devices to tailor the course to individual needs.

Components of *Top Notch 1*

Student's Book with Take-Home Super CD-ROM

The Super CD-ROM includes a variety of exciting interactive activities: Speaking Practice, Interactive Workbook, Games and Puzzles, and *Top Notch Pop* Karaoke. The disk can also be played on an audio CD player to listen to the Conversation Models and the *Top Notch Pop* songs.

Teacher's Edition with Daily Lesson Plans

Complete yet concise lesson plans are provided for each class. Corpus notes provide essential information from the *Longman Spoken American Corpus* and the *Longman Learner's Corpus*. In addition, a free Teacher's Resource Disk offers the following printable extension activities to personalize your teaching style:

- Grammar self-checks
- *Top Notch Pop* song activities
- Writing process worksheets
- Learning strategies
- Pronunciation activities and supplements
- Extra reading comprehension activities
- Vocabulary cards and cumulative vocabulary activities
- Graphic organizers
- Pair work cards

Copy & Go: Ready-made Interactive Activities for Busy Teachers

Interactive games, puzzles, and other practice activities in convenient photocopiable form support the Student's Book content and provide a welcome change of pace.

Complete Classroom Audio Program

The audio program, available in cassette or audio CD format, contains listening comprehension activities, rhythm and intonation practice, and targeted pronunciation activities that focus on accurate and comprehensible pronunciation.

Because *Top Notch* prepares students for international communication, a variety of native and non-native speakers are included to ready students for the world outside the classroom. The audio program also includes the five *Top Notch Pop* songs in standard and karaoke form.

Workbook

A tightly linked illustrated Workbook contains exercises that provide additional practice and reinforcement of language concepts and skills from *Top Notch* and its Grammar Booster.

Complete Assessment Package with *ExamView®* Software

Ten easy-to-administer and easy-to-score unit achievement tests assess listening, vocabulary, grammar, social language, reading, and writing. Two review tests, one mid-book and one end-of-book, provide additional cumulative assessment. Two speaking tests assess progress in speaking. In addition to the photocopiable achievement tests, *ExamView®* software enables teachers to tailor-make tests to best meet their needs by combining items in any way they wish.

Top Notch TV

A lively and entertaining video offers a TV-style situation comedy that reintroduces language from each *Top Notch* unit, plus authentic unrehearsed interviews with English speakers from around the world and authentic karaoke. Packaged with the video are activity worksheets, and a booklet with teaching suggestions and complete video scripts.

Companion Website

A Companion Website at www.longman.com/topnotch provides numerous additional resources for students and teachers. This no-cost, high-benefit feature includes opportunities for further practice of language and content from the *Top Notch* Student's Book.

About the Authors

Joan Saslow

Joan Saslow has taught English as a Foreign Language and English as a Second Language to adults and young adults in both South America and the United States. She taught English and French at the Binational Centers of Valparaíso and Viña del Mar, Chile, and the Catholic University of Valparaíso. In the United States, Ms. Saslow taught English as a Foreign Language to Japanese university students at Marymount College and to international students in Westchester Community College's intensive English program as well as workplace English at the General Motors auto assembly plant in Tarrytown, NY.

Ms. Saslow is the series director of Longman's popular five-level adult series ***True Colors: An EFL Course for Real Communication*** and of ***True Voices***, a five-level video course. She is author of ***Ready to Go: Language, Lifeskills, and Civics***, a four-level adult ESL series; ***Workplace Plus***, a vocational English series; and of ***Literacy Plus***, a two-level series that teaches literacy, English, and culture to adult pre-literate students. She is also author of ***English in Context: Reading Comprehension for Science and Technology***, a three-level series for English for special purposes. In addition, Ms. Saslow has been an author, an editor of language teaching materials, a teacher-trainer, and a frequent speaker at gatherings of EFL and ESL teachers for over thirty years.

Allen Ascher

Allen Ascher has been a teacher and teacher-trainer in both China and the United States, as well as an administrator and a publisher. Mr. Ascher specialized in teaching listening and speaking to students at the Beijing Second Foreign Language Institute, to hotel workers at a major international hotel in China, and to Japanese students from Chubu University studying English at Ohio University. In New York, Mr. Ascher taught students of all language backgrounds and abilities at the City University of New York, and he trained teachers in the TESOL Certificate Program at the New School. He was also the academic director of the International English Language Institute at Hunter College.

Mr. Ascher has provided lively workshops for EFL teachers throughout Asia, Latin America, Europe, and the Middle East. He is author of the popular ***Think about Editing: A Grammar Editing Guide for ESL Writers***. As a publisher, Mr. Ascher played a key role in the creation of some of the most widely used materials for adults, including: ***True Colors, NorthStar, Focus on Grammar, Global Links***, and ***Ready to Go***. Mr. Ascher has an M.A. in Applied Linguistics from Ohio University.

UNIT 6

Staying in Shape

UNIT GOALS

1 Plan an activity with someone
2 Talk about daily routines
3 Discuss exercise and diet
4 Describe your typical day

A TOPIC PREVIEW. Look at the graphs. Which activities do you do regularly?

How Many Calories Can a Person* BURN IN ONE HOUR?

*Based on a person weighing 150 pounds/68.2 kilograms.

PHYSICAL ACTIVITIES

Number of calories burned

lift weights	214
go walking	250
go dancing	322
play golf	322
do aerobics	429
go bike riding	500
play tennis	501
play soccer	501
go swimming	572
go running	572
play basketball	572

EVERYDAY ACTIVITIES

Number of calories burned

sleep	64
watch TV	71
read	71
talk on the phone	71
work in an office	107
study English	128
go shopping	164
cook dinner	179
clean the house	179
play the guitar	214
take a shower	248

SOURCE: www.msnbc.com

B VOCABULARY. Activities. Listen and practice.

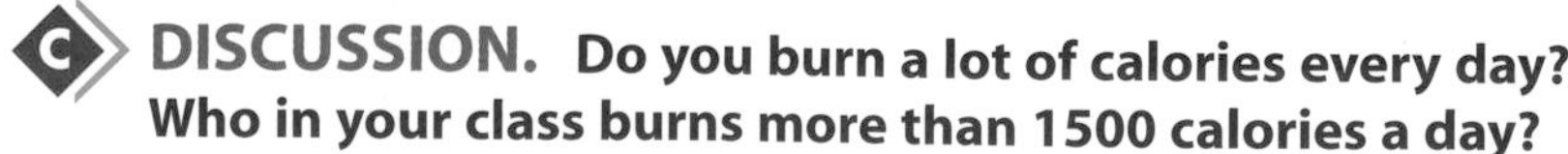

C DISCUSSION. Do you burn a lot of calories every day? Who in your class burns more than 1500 calories a day?

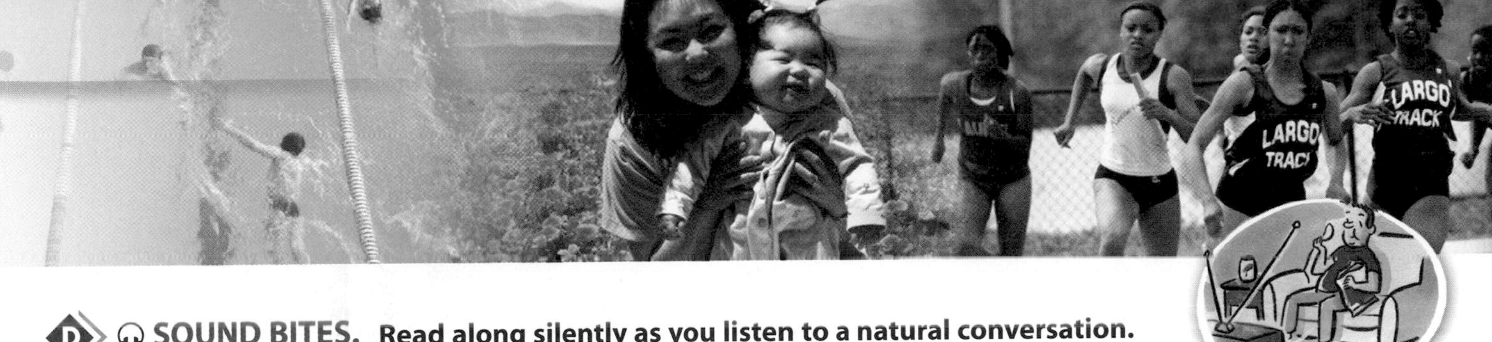

D SOUND BITES. Read along silently as you listen to a natural conversation.

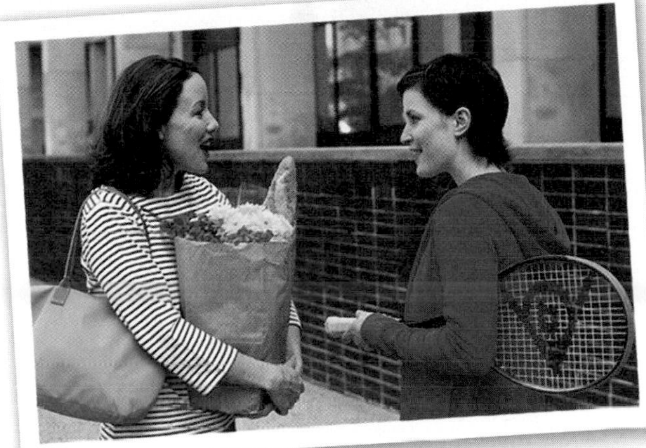

SUE: Hey, Jane! Where are you off to?

JANE: I'm on my way to the park.

SUE: You play tennis? How often?

JANE: Just about every weekend. Do you want to play together sometime?

SUE: That would be great.

SUE: What about your husband? Does he play?

JANE: Ed? No way. He's a couch potato.

SUE: Too bad. My husband's crazy about tennis.

E UNDERSTANDING MEANING FROM CONTEXT. Use the conversation to help you choose the correct response.

1. "Where are you off to?"
   - ☐ I'm going to work.
   - ☐ I play tennis.
2. "Do you lift weights?"
   - ☐ No kidding.
   - ☐ No way.
3. "Does your daughter play golf?"
   - ☐ Yes. She's crazy about golf.
   - ☐ Yes. She's a couch potato.
4. "How often do you play tennis?"
   - ☐ Well, let's play together some time.
   - ☐ I don't. I'm a couch potato.

WHAT ABOUT **YOU?**

Write about your activities.

Every day	Every weekend	Once a week	Once in a while	Never
I study English.				

LESSON

1 Plan an Activity with Someone

CONVERSATION MODEL Read and listen.

A: Hey, Paul. Why don't we play basketball sometime?
B: Great idea. When's good for you?
A: Tomorrow at three?
B: Sorry, I can't. I have to meet my sister at the airport.
A: How about Wednesday at five?
B: That sounds great.

Rhythm and intonation practice

A GRAMMAR. Can and have to

can

Use can + the base form of a verb for ability or possibility.

I **can speak** English, but I **can't speak** Italian.
I **can't play** golf today. I'm too busy.

Yes / no questions	**Short answers**
Can you **come** for dinner this evening?	Yes, I can. / No, I can't.

can't = can not / cannot

have to

Use have to + the base form of a verb for obligation.

I can't go running tomorrow. I **have to meet** my cousin after class.
She can't come for dinner. She **has to work** late.
Dave can sleep late. He **doesn't have to go** to work.
Relax! You **don't have to drive** to the airport until 10:00.

Yes / no questions	**Short answers**
Do you **have to work** tomorrow?	Yes, I do. / No, I don't.
Does she **have to go** to school today?	Yes, she does. / No, she doesn't.

don't = do not
doesn't = does not

PAGES G10–G12
For more . . .

B Complete the sentences with can or have to.

1. Vicky ________ (not / come) for dinner tonight. She ________ (finish) a report for her boss.
2. I ________ (meet) you at 6:00. I ________ (not / work) late tonight.
3. My brother ________ (not / play) soccer today. He ________ (go) to the doctor.
4. I want to see a movie, but I have an exam tomorrow. I ________ (study) tonight.
5. ________ Nick ________ (play) golf with us next Wednesday?

C PRONUNCIATION. Can / can't. Listen to the pronunciation and stress of can and can't in sentences. Then listen again and repeat.

/kən/	/kænt/
I can **call** you tomorrow.	I **can't** call you tomorrow.

Now listen carefully and check can or can't. Then listen again and repeat.

1. ☐ can ☐ can't
2. ☐ can ☐ can't
3. ☐ can ☐ can't
4. ☐ can ☐ can't
5. ☐ can ☐ can't
6. ☐ can ☐ can't

D PAIR WORK. Write three invitations using can. Then read your partner's invitations and write excuses.

Can you go swimming tomorrow?

Sorry, I can't. I have to work.

CONVERSATION PAIR WORK

Write your schedule for this weekend in the daily planner.

	FRIDAY	SATURDAY	SUNDAY
9:00	go running	visit Mom	

GROUP WORK. Talk to at least three different classmates. Plan an activity together this weekend. Use your daily planner.

A: _____. Why don't we _____ sometime?
B: Great idea. When's good for you?
A: _____?
B: _____ ...

Continue the conversation in your own way.

Daily Planner

	FRIDAY	SATURDAY	SUNDAY
9:00			
11:00			
1:00			
3:00			
5:00			
7:00			

LESSON

2 Talk about Daily Routines

CONVERSATION MODEL Read and listen.

A: Janet! What are you doing here?
B: Hi, Lisa. I always go to the gym on Saturday morning. You too?
A: Actually, I usually go in the evening. But not today.
B: How come?
A: I'm going to the theater tonight.
B: Well, have a great time.

Rhythm and intonation practice

A GRAMMAR. The simple present tense and the present continuous

The simple present tense

Use the simple present tense to describe frequency, habits, and routines.

How often **do** you **play** basketball? — I **play** basketball at least once a week.
When **does** Paula **do** aerobics? — She **does** aerobics on Tuesdays.
When **do** you usually **go** to the gym? — I usually **go** in the evening.

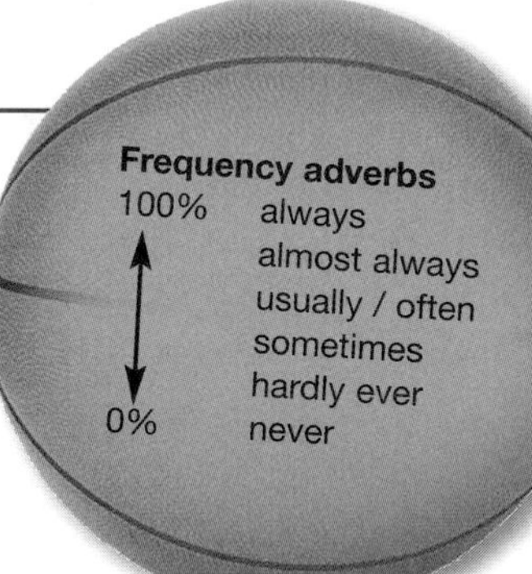

The present continuous

Use the present continuous for actions in progress now or for future plans.

She**'s talking** on the phone. — Paul and Judy **are going** running tomorrow.

Don't use the present continuous with frequency adverbs.
Don't say: ~~She's usually talking on the phone~~.
Don't use the present continuous with have, want, need, or like.
Don't say: ~~She's liking the gym~~.

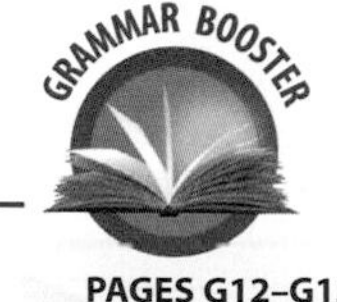

PAGES G12–G13 For more . . .

B Complete the sentences. Use the simple present tense or the present continuous.

1. How often ________ (you / go) running?
2. I'm sorry. ________ (Paul / study) right now.
3. ________ (I / go) to the track this afternoon.
4. ________ (I / lift) weights three times a week.
5. ________ (Tim / cook) lunch. Can he call you back?
6. How often ________ (you / play) the guitar?
7. ________ (I / play) tennis every day.

C VOCABULARY. Places for physical activities. Listen and practice.

a park

a gym

a track

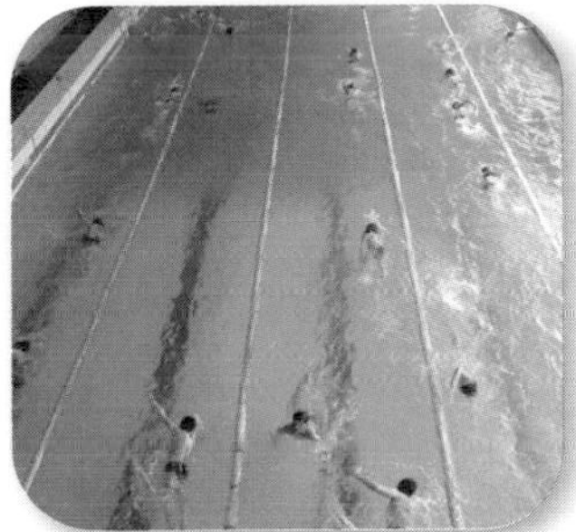
a pool

an athletic field

a golf course

a tennis court

D LISTENING COMPREHENSION. Listen to each conversation. Match the conversation with the place.

__f__ 1.	a. a park
_____ 2.	b. a gym
_____ 3.	c. a track
_____ 4.	d. a pool
_____ 5.	e. an athletic field
_____ 6.	f. a golf course
_____ 7.	g. a tennis court

CONVERSATION PAIR WORK

Talk about daily routines. Use the guide, or create a new conversation.

A: _____! What are you doing here?
B: Hi, _____. I always _____ on _____. You too?
A: Actually, I usually _____. But not today.
B: How come?
A: _____ . . .

Continue the conversation in your own way.

CONTROLLED PRACTICE

LESSON 3

Discuss Exercise and Diet

A VOCABULARY. Talking about health habits. Listen and practice.

be in shape

be out of shape

eat junk food

avoid sweets

have a sweet tooth

B Practice the new vocabulary. Complete each statement.

1. I hardly ever exercise, and I usually don't feel healthy. I'm really _____.
   a. in great shape **b.** out of shape **c.** a sweet tooth
2. I generally try to eat healthy foods. I avoid _____.
   a. fatty foods **b.** vegetables **c.** fruits
3. My son has a real sweet tooth. He loves _____.
   a. fish **b.** candy **c.** meat

LISTENING COMPREHENSION. Listen to people talk about their health habits. Then listen again and check the statements that are true.

1. Juan Reyneri:

- ☐ generally eats small meals.
- ☐ generally eats large meals.
- ☐ usually drinks soft drinks.
- ☐ usually drinks a lot of water.
- ☐ exercises regularly.
- ☐ doesn't exercise regularly.

2. Naomi Sato:

- ☐ exercises regularly.
- ☐ doesn't exercise regularly.
- ☐ eats fish once a week.
- ☐ hardly ever eats fish.
- ☐ eats fruits and vegetables every day.
- ☐ hardly ever eats fruits and vegetables.

3. Matt Lemke:

- ☐ exercises regularly.
- ☐ doesn't exercise regularly.
- ☐ generally avoids fatty foods.
- ☐ doesn't avoid fatty foods.
- ☐ always drinks a lot of water.
- ☐ always drinks soft drinks.

PRONUNCIATION. Third-person singular -s. Listen. Then repeat.

/s/	/z/	/ɪz/
sleeps	goes	watches
eats	plays	exercises
works	avoids	munches

TOP NOTCH INTERACTION • *Are You a Couch Potato?*

STEP 1. **Take the health survey.**

TOP NOTCH HEALTH SURVEY

Check the statements that are true for you. Then add up your total score.

1. ☐ **a.** I exercise regularly.
   ☐ **b.** I don't have time to exercise regularly.
   ☐ **c.** I don't want to exercise regularly.
2. ☐ **a.** I always get enough sleep.
   ☐ **b.** I sometimes don't get enough sleep.
   ☐ **c.** I never get enough sleep.
3. ☐ **a.** I always eat vegetables.
   ☐ **b.** I sometimes eat vegetables.
   ☐ **c.** I never eat vegetables.
4. ☐ **a.** I avoid fatty foods.
   ☐ **b.** I sometimes eat fatty foods.
   ☐ **c.** I eat lots of fatty foods.
5. ☐ **a.** I hardly ever eat sweets.
   ☐ **b.** I sometimes eat sweets.
   ☐ **c.** I have a sweet tooth.

Score

Each **a** answer = 10 points.
Each **b** answer = 5 points.
Each **c** answer = 0 points.

Total points: ☐

40–50 points = You're in terrific shape!

30–35 points = Not bad. Keep it up!

20–25 points = Come on. Try harder!

0–15 points = You're a couch potato!

STEP 2. PAIR WORK. Compare your survey answers and scores. Then compare your exercise and diet habits.

"Do you exercise at home? How often?"

STEP 3. PAIR WORK. Walk around your classroom and ask questions. Write your classmates' names on the chart.

Find someone who …	Name
1. eats a lot of junk food.	
2. lifts weights regularly.	
3. doesn't have time to exercise.	
4. exercises at home.	
5. never eats sweets.	
6. doesn't get enough sleep every night.	
7. goes running regularly.	

STEP 4. GROUP WORK. Tell your class about some of your classmates.

"Frank exercises at home every day."

Describe Your Typical Day

LESSON

 **READING WARM-UP.** **Look at the photo. What do you think is the relationship between the two women? What do you think they are doing?**

 **READING.** **Read the article about Brooke Ellison. How is her day different from yours?**

With her mother's help, Brooke Ellison remains active

In June 2000, Brooke Ellison graduated from Harvard University. And now she is continuing her studies as a full-time graduate student. Brooke is a quadriplegic—she can't move her arms or legs. She spends all her time in a wheelchair, and she can't breathe without a special machine. A terrible accident at the age of 11 changed her life—she was hit by a car on her way home from school. But she stays active every day.

On a typical morning, it takes most people about a half hour to get up, get dressed, and have breakfast. For Brooke, it usually takes about four hours. Her mother, Jean, wakes her early in the morning and exercises her arms and legs. Then she gives her a bath, combs her hair, and brushes her teeth. After that, she dresses her and lifts her into her wheelchair. By late morning, Brooke is ready for breakfast. In the afternoon, Brooke goes to her classes and listens carefully. Her mother goes to classes with her and takes notes. For a lot of activities, such as using a calculator, Brooke uses her mouth, instead of her hands and legs. She can move her wheelchair by blowing into a tube.

At night, she does her homework and reads her e-mail, and she often phones her brother or sister to talk. To use a computer, she uses her voice—she tells the computer what to do. At about 8:00, she gets ready for bed—it usually takes about two hours. Her mother undresses her, bathes her, and exercises her arms and legs again.

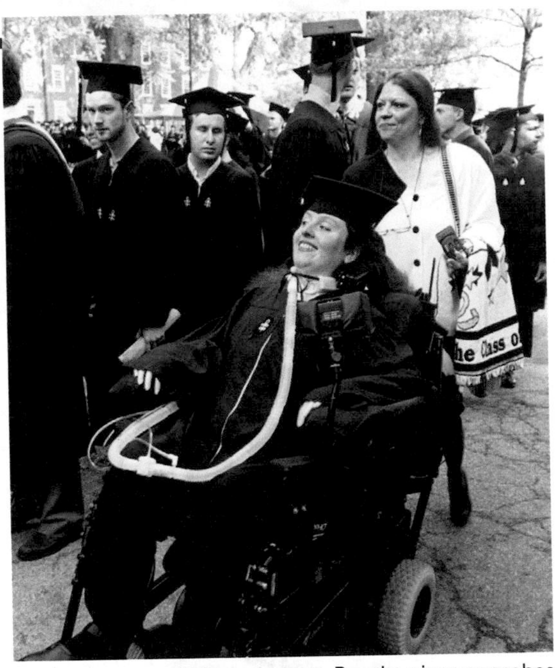

When she can, Brooke gives speeches to young people. She tells them about her life and teaches them to always be active.

SOURCES: *Miracles Happen*, Brooke and Jean Ellison, 2001, Hyperion and *The Brooke Ellison Story*, directed by Christopher Reeve, 2004

C **Read the article again. Complete each statement with <u>can</u>, <u>can't</u>, or <u>has to</u>.**

Brooke Ellison:

1. ___can't___ walk.
2. __________ use a wheelchair.
3. __________ breathe without a special machine.
4. __________ get up early every day.
5. __________ use a computer.
6. __________ use a calculator.
7. __________ use her hands.
8. __________ read her e-mail.

D Write what Brooke and Jean Ellison do each day.

In the morning: Brooke gets up early. Jean combs her hair.
____
____

In the afternoon: ____________________
____
____

In the evening: ____________________
____
____

TOP NOTCH INTERACTION • *What About You?*

STEP 1. Answer the questions about your typical day.

1. What time do you usually get up? ____________________.
2. What do you do next? ____________________.
3. Do you usually eat breakfast? ____________________.
4. When do you usually have lunch? ____________________.
5. What do you do in the evening? ____________________.
6. What time do you go to bed? ____________________.

STEP 2. PAIR WORK. Interview a partner about his or her activities on a typical day. Use some or all of the questions in Step 1. Take notes on the notepad.

In the morning	In the afternoon	In the evening

STEP 3. DISCUSSION. Tell your class about your partner's typical day.

STEP 4. WRITING. Write an article about your partner's typical day.

In the morning, Nina usually gets up early and goes running. After that, she eats breakfast. She usually has cereal and juice. After breakfast...

FREE PRACTICE

UNIT 6 CHECKPOINT

A LISTENING COMPREHENSION. **Listen carefully. Check ☑ the box to complete each statement. Then listen again to check your work.**

1. She ___ eats breakfast. ☐ usually ☐ never ☐ almost always
2. Tony ___ goes swimming on Mondays. ☐ usually ☐ never ☐ hardly ever
3. He ___ eats healthy food. ☐ never ☐ almost always ☐ hardly ever
4. She goes running ___. ☐ daily ☐ once in a while ☐ three times a week

B **What physical activities can you do in each of these places? Write sentences.**

an athletic field	a gym	a park
I can play soccer.	______	______
______	______	______
______	______	______

C **Choose the best response.**

1. "Why don't we go to the pool next week?"
   ☐ Well, have a great time.
   ☐ Sorry, I can't. I have to study.
2. "Why don't we have dinner together tonight? How about at eight?"
   ☐ When's good for you?
   ☐ Sure. Sounds great.
3. "What are you doing here?"
   ☐ Sorry, I can't.
   ☐ I always have lunch here on Saturdays.

TOP NOTCH SONG
"A Typical Day"
Lyrics on last page before Workbook.

TOP NOTCH PROJECT
Vote to decide the five most important health habits. Make a poster for your class.

TOP NOTCH WEBSITE
For Unit 6 online activities, visit the *Top Notch* Companion Website at www.longman.com/topnotch.

D **Answer the questions with real information.**

1. How often do you go to your English class? YOU ______.
2. Are you going to your English class tomorrow? YOU ______.
3. What do you usually do on weekends? YOU ______.
4. What are you doing this weekend? YOU ______.

E WRITING. **Write about your typical day.**

Every morning, I get up at 6:30. I usually take a shower and ...

Unit Wrap-Up

- **Vocabulary and grammar.** Talk about how often you do the activities in the picture.
- **Social language.** Create a conversation for the two men.
- **Writing.** Write about the people.
  A woman is cooking.

Now I can . . .

- ☐ plan an activity with someone.
- ☐ talk about daily routines.
- ☐ discuss exercise and diet.
- ☐ describe my typical day.

UNIT 7

Finding Something to Wear

UNIT GOALS

1 Shop for clothes
2 Pay for clothes
3 Give and get directions in a store
4 Discuss culturally appropriate dress

A TOPIC PREVIEW. Look at the store website. What department would you click on?

B DISCUSSION. Where do you shop for clothes? Do you ever shop online?

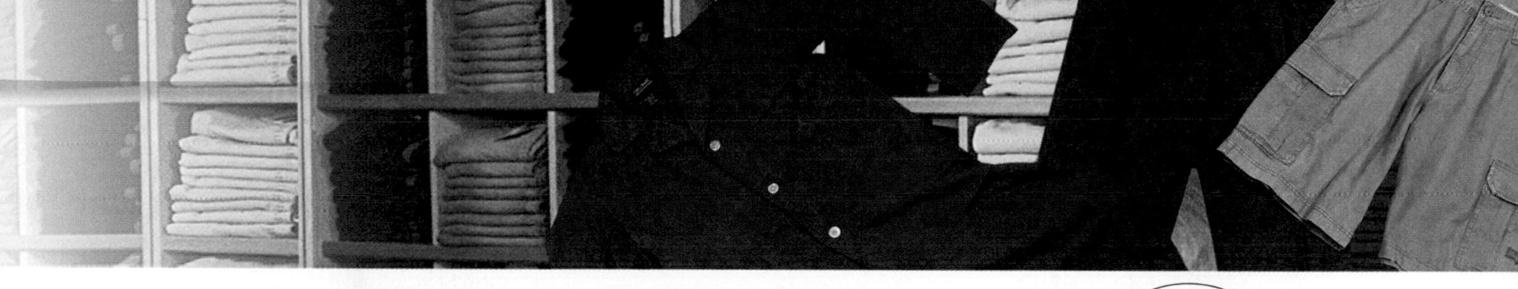

C SOUND BITES. **Read along silently as you listen to a natural conversation.**

SHOPPER: Excuse me. How much is that V-neck?

CLERK: This red one? It's $55.

SHOPPER: That's not too bad. And it's really nice.

SHOPPER: Do you have it in a larger size?

CLERK: Here you go. This one's a medium. Would you like to try it on?

SHOPPER: No, thanks. It's for my sister. Would you be nice enough to gift wrap it for me?

CLERK: Of course!

D **Read the conversation carefully and check ☑ the statements that are true. Then explain your answers.**

- ☐ **1.** The clerk asks about the price.
- ☐ **2.** The first sweater is the right size.
- ☐ **3.** The sweater is a gift.
- ☐ **4.** The shopper buys the sweater.

E UNDERSTANDING MEANING FROM CONTEXT. **Complete the statements.**

1. When the shopper says, "Excuse me," she means _____.
   a. Can you help me? **b.** I don't understand.
2. When the shopper says, "That's not too bad," she means _____.
   a. The sweater is nice. **b.** The price is not too high.
3. When the clerk says, "Here you go," she means _____.
   a. Here's a cheaper one. **b.** Here's a larger one.

WHAT ABOUT **YOU?**

What's important to you when you choose a place to shop for clothes? Complete the chart.

	Not important	Important	Very important
Prices	○	○	○
Brands	○	○	○
Selection	○	○	○
Service	○	○	○

PAIR WORK. **Compare your opinions.**

LESSON

1 Shop for Clothes

CONVERSATION MODEL Read and listen.

A: Excuse me. Do you have these gloves in a larger size?
B: No, I'm sorry. We don't.
A: That's too bad.
B: But we have a larger pair in brown. See if they are better.
A: Yes, they're fine. Thanks.

 **Rhythm and intonation practice**

A GRAMMAR. Comparative adjectives

small → small**er**	large → large**r**	heavy → heav**ier**	big → big**ger**
cheap → cheap**er**	loose → loose**r**	pretty → prett**ier**	hot → hot**ter**

Irregular forms
good → better
bad → worse

Use comparative adjectives to compare two people, places, or things.

Do you have these pants in a **larger** size? This pair is too tight.

Use more or less with adjectives that have two or more syllables and don't end in -y.

Do you have a **more comfortable** pair of shoes?
Let's look for a **less expensive** suit.

Use than after the adjective when you compare two items.

Some people say that black is more flattering **than** white, but white looks better on me.

PAGES G13–G14
For more . . .

B Complete each conversation with comparative adjectives. Use than if necessary.

1. **A:** I just love these gloves, but I wish they were warmer (warm).
   B: What about these? They look great, and they're much ______ (expensive).
2. **A:** Don't take those pajamas to Hawaii! It's hot there. Take something ______ (light).
   B: Good idea.
3. **A:** What do you think of this red dress?
   B: Beautiful. It's ______ (pretty) the black one. And ______ (cheap), too.
4. **A:** Excuse me. Do these pants come in a ______ (long) length? These are too short.
   B: Let me see if I can find you something ______ (good).

C VOCABULARY. Clothing described as "pairs." Listen and practice.

(a pair of) gloves

(a pair of) pajamas

(a pair of) socks

(a pair of) panties

(a pair of) boxers
(a pair of) briefs

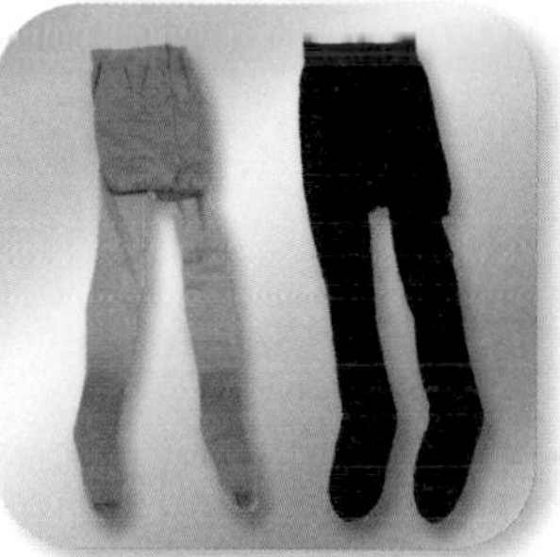
(a pair of) pantyhose
(a pair of) tights

(a pair of) pants
(a pair of) shorts

D LISTENING COMPREHENSION. Circle the clothing discussed in each conversation.

1. stockings — (gloves)
2. boxers — pajamas
3. tights — gloves
4. pajamas — boxers
5. pantyhose — panties

CONVERSATION PAIR WORK

Role-play shopping for clothes. Start like this:

Excuse me.
Do you have ____?

Continue the conversation in your own way . . .

Ideas
in a smaller size
in a larger size
in another color
in [black]
in size [34]

LESSON

2 Pay for Clothes

CONVERSATION MODEL Read and listen.

A: I'll take the loafers.
B: Certainly. How would you like to pay for them?
A: Excuse me?
B: Cash or charge?
A: Charge, please. And could you gift wrap them for me?
B: Absolutely.

Rhythm and intonation practice

A VOCABULARY. Types of clothing and shoes. Listen and practice.

casual clothes

① jeans ② a T-shirt
③ a sweatshirt ④ a polo shirt
⑤ sweatpants

sweaters and jackets

① a crew neck ② a cardigan
③ a turtleneck ④ a V-neck
⑤ a windbreaker ⑥ a blazer

shoes

① oxfords ② loafers
③ sandals ④ running shoes
⑤ pumps ⑥ flats

B GRAMMAR. Uses of object pronouns

As direct objects

I want **the sweatshirt**. → I want **it**.
I love **these jeans**. → I love **them**.

In prepositional phrases

Give this hat **to Jane**. → Give this hat **to her**.
He's buying a bag **for his wife**. → He's buying a bag **for her**.

In sentences with both direct objects and object pronouns, the prepositional phrase comes last.

I want the sweatpants. Can you gift wrap **them for me**?

PAGES G14–G15
For more . . .

C **Underline the direct object in each sentence. Then rewrite the sentence, replacing the direct object with an object pronoun.**

1. They bought the green sweatpants.
   They bought them.
2. I love these windbreakers.
   ______.
3. I'm buying the crew neck.
   ______.
4. Did you see the blue polo shirts?
   ______?
5. I don't need the cardigan.
   ______.
6. Do you still have that great pair of flats?
   ______?
7. They gave the old jackets to us.
   ______.

D **Write the words and phrases in the correct order.**

1. I / it / for her / am buying
   ______.
2. They / them / for us / are getting
   ______.
3. Please / it / to me / give
   ______.
4. for my son-in-law / I / them / need
   ______.
5. it / He / is gift wrapping / for me
   ______.

CONVERSATION PAIR WORK

Role-play paying for clothes. Use the guide, or create a new conversation.

A: I'll take the ______.
B: ______. How would you like to pay for ______?
A: Excuse me?
B: Cash or charge?
A: ______, please. And could you gift wrap ______ for me?
B: ______.

LESSON

3 Give and Get Directions in a Store

A VOCABULARY. Locations and directions. Listen and practice.

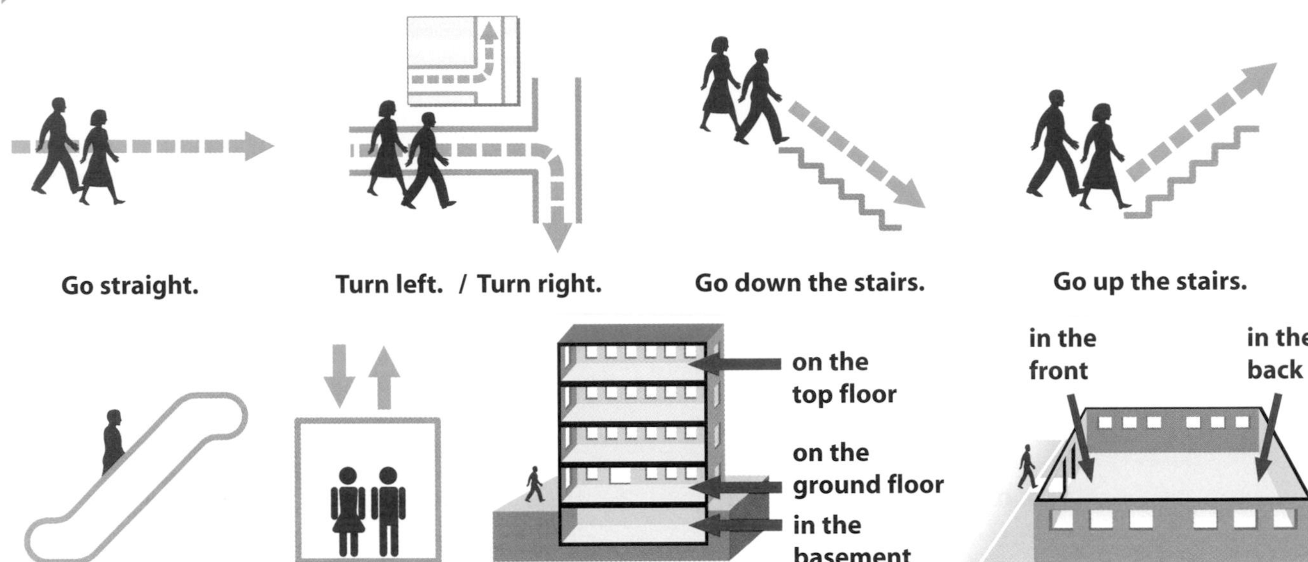

B LISTENING COMPREHENSION. Listen to the directions at an information desk. Then listen again and write the number of each place on the diagrams.

1	Coats	4	Lingerie
2	Children's shoes	5	Accessories
3	Coffee shop		

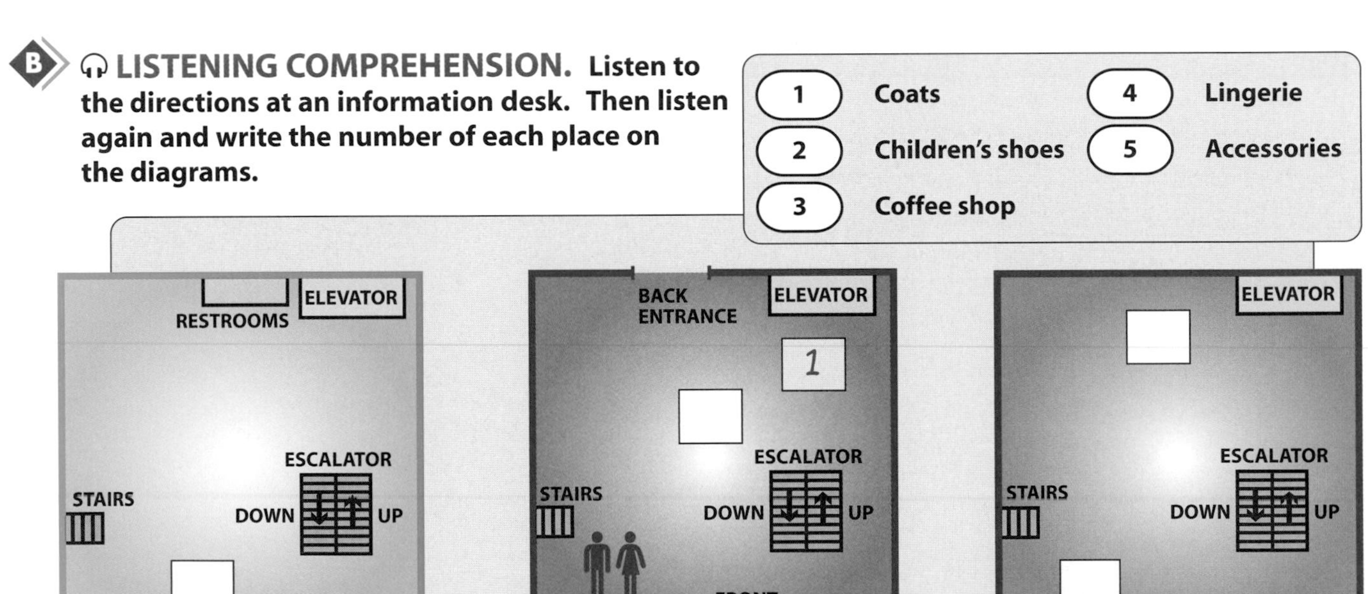

C PRONUNCIATION. Contrastive stress for clarification. Read, listen, and repeat.

A: The shoe department is upstairs, on the third floor.

B: Excuse me? The first floor?

A: No. It's on the third floor.

STEP 1. On the notepad, write things you can find in each department.

Men's:	Lingerie:
Women's:	Electronics:
Shoes:	Appliances:

STEP 2. PAIR WORK. Look at the department store floor plan and store directory. Role-play conversations between a shopper and an information clerk. Use the items on the notepad.

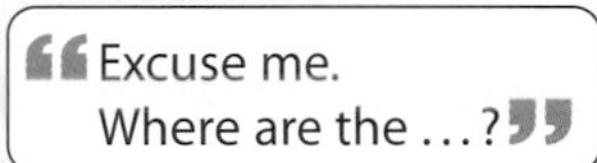

STORE DIRECTORY

Bags and Accessories	Ground Floor
Electronics	Basement
Hosiery	Ground Floor
Lingerie	Ground Floor
Men's Athleticwear	2
Men's Casual	2
Men's Outerwear	2
Men's Shoes	2
Men's Sleepwear	2
Men's Underwear	2
Photo Studio	Basement
Restaurant	Basement
Small Appliances	Basement
Women's Casual	Ground Floor
Women's Shoes	Ground Floor

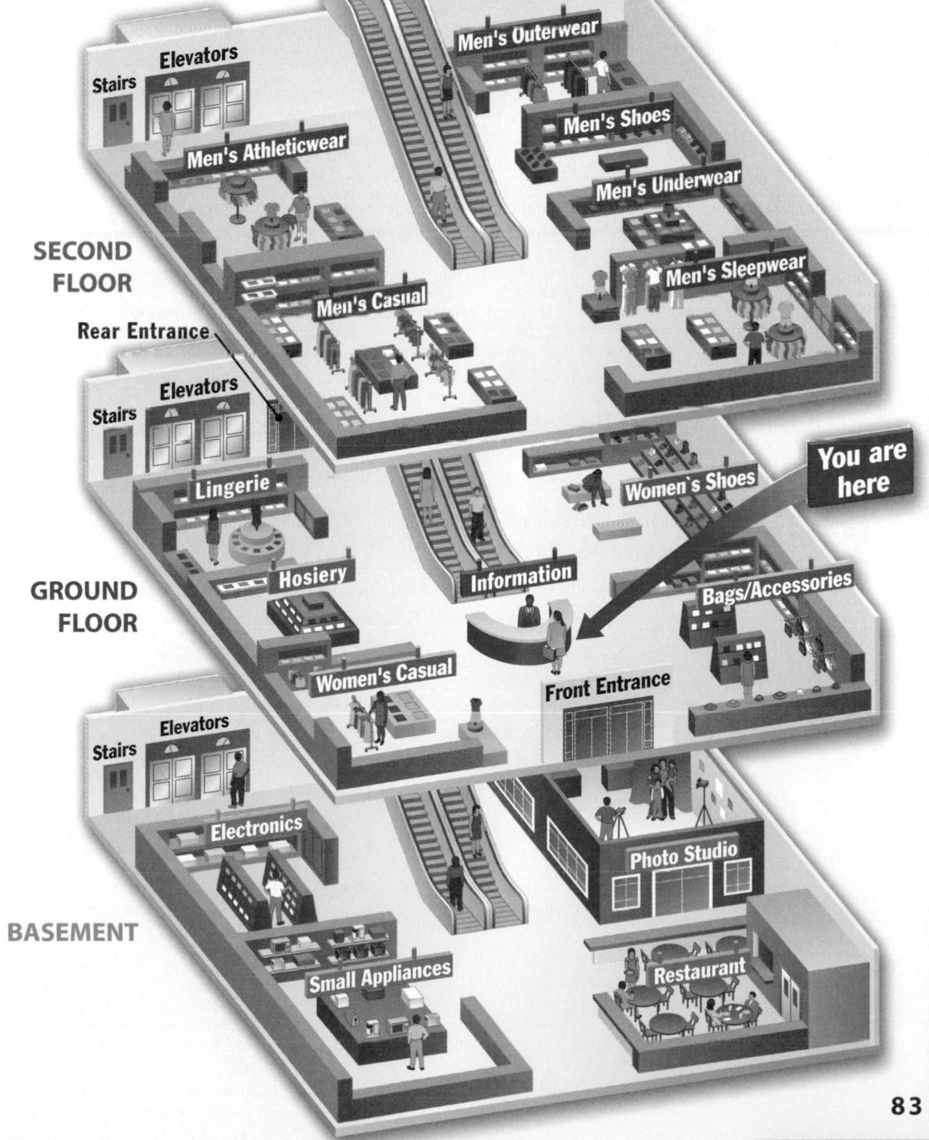

LESSON

4 Discuss Culturally Appropriate Dress

A READING WARM-UP. What do you wear when the weather is warm? —when you want to look informal? —when you need to look more formal?

B READING. Read about clothing do's and don'ts for travelers. Then explain why this information is helpful.

Know before you go . . .

Every culture has unwritten "rules" about appropriate and inappropriate dress. Some cultures have a liberal attitude about clothing, while other cultures are more conservative. Read about some clothing do's and don'ts for three popular travel destinations around the world.

Holland

Holland has a northern climate, so depending on the time of year you're visiting, pack lighter or heavier clothes. One thing people notice about Holland is the way young people dress. Their dress code is "anything goes," so it's not unusual to see some pretty wild clothes there!

Thailand

If you're visiting beautiful Thailand from May to September, pack for the heat. Thailand is generally conservative when it comes to clothing, but at Thailand's magnificent temples, the rules about clothing, and especially shoes, are very strict. If your shoes are too open, they are considered disrespectful, and you will have to change to more modest ones. So be prepared with light but modest clothing and shoes for your Thailand trip.

a Thai temple

an Egyptian mosque

Egypt

Summertime is hot in Egypt, so pack light clothing. But be sure to bring warm-weather clothing that is also modest. If you visit a mosque, shorts are definitely out of the question, for both men and women. In mosques, women should wear longer skirts and a head covering, usually a scarf. And the upper part of their arms should be covered with sleeves. For touring other wonderful sights and historical places, casual, comfortable clothing is fine for both men and women.

SOURCE: *Rough Guide* and *Berlitz* travel guides

C **DISCUSSION.** **Rate the dress code for each country. Then explain each rating you made.**

	conservative		liberal		"anything goes!"
Egypt	✔	○	○	○	○
Holland	○	○	○	○	○
Thailand	○	○	○	○	○
This country	○	○	○	○	○

D **PAIR WORK.** **Plan your clothes for a July visit to one of the following places.**

- an Egyptian mosque
- the pyramids in Egypt
- a casual restaurant in Holland
- a Thai temple

TOP NOTCH INTERACTION • *Do's and Don'ts*

STEP 1. **Take the opinion survey.**

What's your personal dress code?

Circle "agree" or "disagree" for each statement about clothing.

It's OK to wear shorts on the street.	agree	disagree
It's OK for men to wear shorts on the street, but not for women.	agree	disagree
It's essential for men to wear a tie in the office.	agree	disagree
It's OK for women to wear pants in the office.	agree	disagree
It's OK for young people to be less conservative in clothing than adults.	agree	disagree
It's essential for women to cover their heads in public.	agree	disagree

How would you rate yourself?

☐ conservative ☐ liberal ☐ "anything goes!"

STEP 2. **On the notepad, write some clothing do's and don'ts for visitors to this country.**

in offices and formal restaurants:

in casual social settings:

in religious institutions:

STEP 3. **GROUP WORK.** **Discuss the do's and don'ts for appropriate dress in this country. Does everyone agree?**

UNIT 7
CHECKPOINT

A LISTENING COMPREHENSION. Listen critically to the conversations about clothes. Infer the name of the department where the people are talking.

Outerwear	Lingerie	Hosiery	Bags and accessories	Shoes

1. ________
2. ________
3. ________
4. ________
5. ________

B Complete each sentence about clothes with an appropriate word.

1. Two kinds of men's underwear are boxers and ________.
2. Two kinds of leg coverings for women are pantyhose and ________.
3. Sandals are a kind of ________.
4. A windbreaker is a kind of ________.
5. You can't buy just one glove. You have to buy a ________.

C Complete the travel article with the comparative form of each adjective.

When you travel, think carefully about the clothes you pack. As far as color is concerned, ________ (1. dark) colors are usually ________ (2. practical). For ________ (3. cool) destinations, a blazer can be ________ (4. convenient) than a windbreaker or cardigan because you can wear it in ________ (5. conservative) settings such as offices and ________ (6. formal) restaurants. For travel to ________ (7. hot) areas of the world, ________ (8. light) clothes are ________ (9. comfortable) than ________ (10. heavy) ones.

***TOP NOTCH* PROJECT**
As a group, write a short entry about this country to the travel guide on page 84. Use your survey, your notepad, and the article as a model.

***TOP NOTCH* WEBSITE**
For Unit 7 online activities, visit the *Top Notch* Companion Website at www.longman.com/topnotch.

D Unscramble each sentence.

1. Please / to me / them / show ________.
2. They / to us / are sending / it ________.
3. When / you / are / to her / it / giving ________?
4. with you / Take / it ________.

E WRITING. Imagine you are taking a trip to another country. On a separate sheet of paper, write about where you are going and what you are going to pack. Explain why. Talk about the climate and the culture.

Unit Wrap-Up

- **Vocabulary.** Look at the picture. Then close your book and write the names of the clothing you remember.
- **Social language.** Create conversations for the people. Use the directory.
- **Grammar.** Write comparisons.
  The blazer is more formal than the windbreaker.

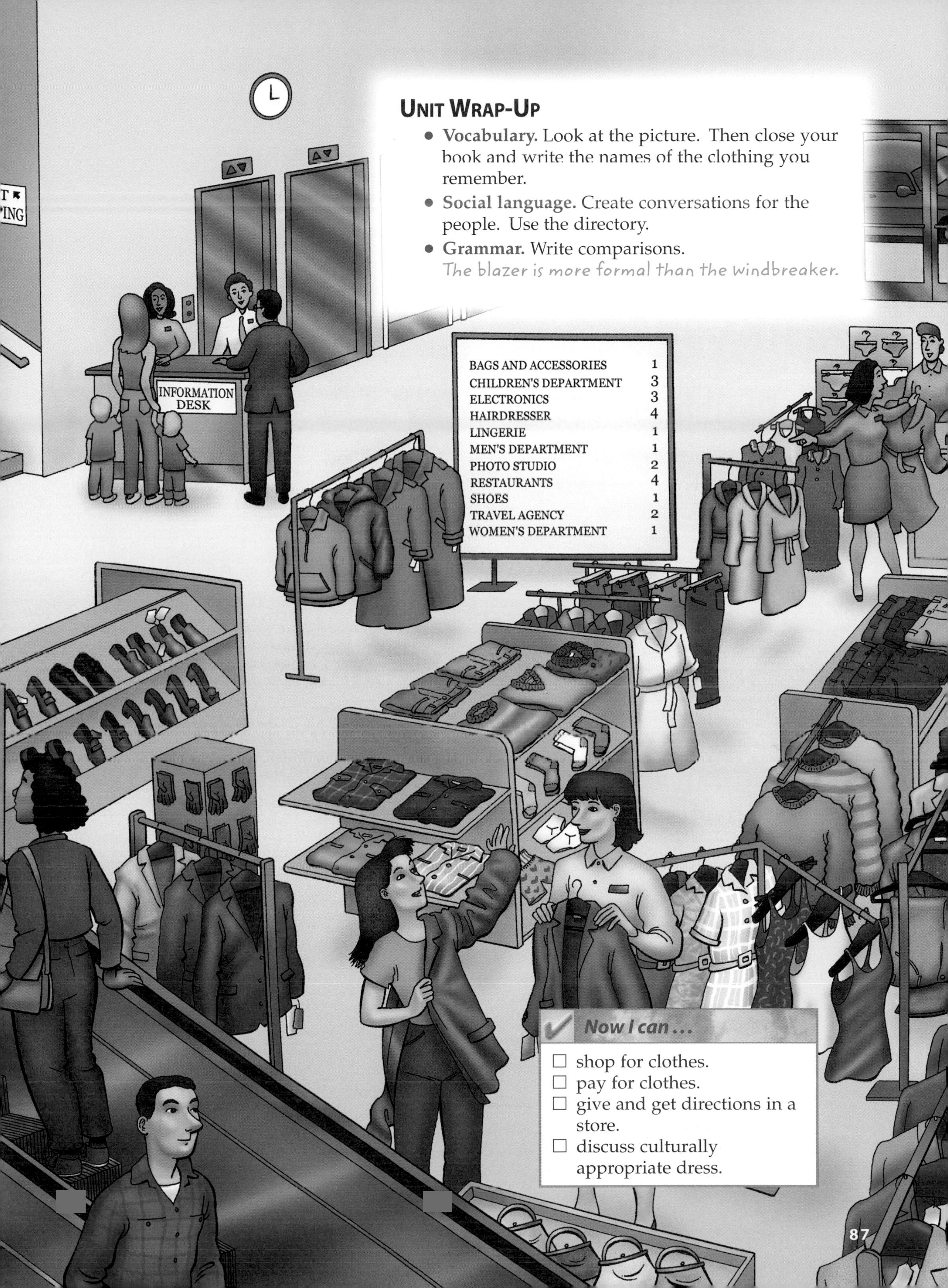

Now I can ...

- ☐ shop for clothes.
- ☐ pay for clothes.
- ☐ give and get directions in a store.
- ☐ discuss culturally appropriate dress.

UNIT 8

Getting Away

UNIT GOALS

1 Greet someone arriving from a trip
2 Talk about how you spent your free time
3 Discuss vacation preferences
4 Tell about your experiences on a trip

TOPIC PREVIEW. Look at the travel ads. Which vacations look good to you? Why?

TRAVEL SPECIALS

10 NIGHT Caribbean Cruise

Departs from / Returns to Miami

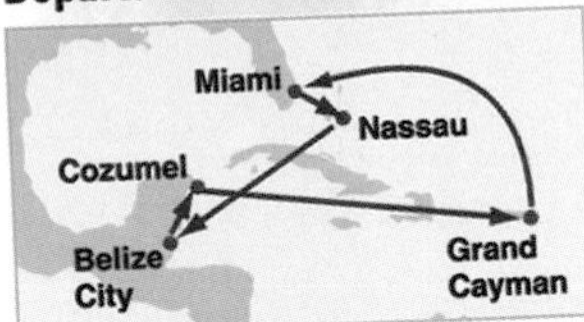

Enjoy snorkeling in **Grand Cayman Island**

Go scuba diving in **Belize**

Play with dolphins in **Nassau**

WHAT'S INCLUDED?

✔ Accommodations ✔ Beverages
✔ Meals ✔ Entertainment

ITALY in Six Days!

You'll savor every minute you spend in romantic Italy!

ROME
Discover the Eternal City! Rome is filled with history and romance.

VENICE
Visit historic St. Mark's Square. And don't miss a gondola voyage on the Grand Canal!

Walt Disney World Resorts®

Disney MGM STUDIOS *Magic Kingdom®*

Something for everyone in your family!

FOUR different theme parks, THREE water parks, shopping, dining, and entertainment.

Choose from over 40 great hotels.

Fly-in African Safari

THE SERENGETI NATIONAL PARK

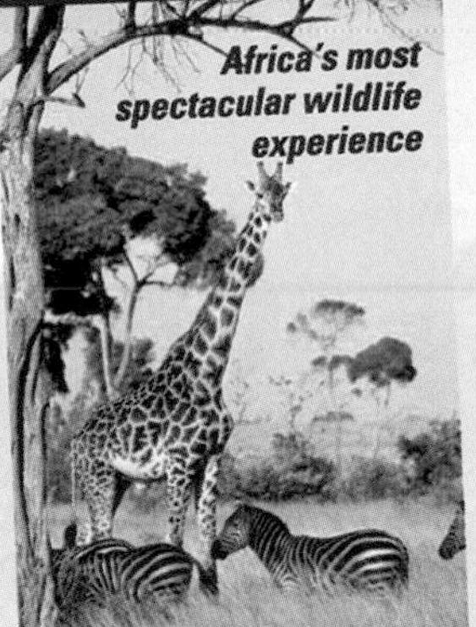

YOU'LL NEVER FORGET IT!

Duration:
3 days/2 nights
Type: Safari fly-in
Country: Tanzania
Rates (US$):
Available on request
Activities include:
Birdwatching, wildlife viewing

SOURCE: Adapted from www.celebritycruises.com; www.ilove-italy.com; www.ineedavacation.com; www.go2africa.com

B DISCUSSION. In your opinion, which of the vacations are good for people who like:

- nature and wildlife?
- family activities?
- history and culture?
- physical activities?

C SOUND BITES. Read along silently as you listen to a natural conversation.

GREG: Hi, Barbara. When did you get back?
BARBARA: Greg! Just yesterday.
GREG: So tell me about your trip.
BARBARA: It was incredible. I had a really great time.
GREG: Good weather?
BARBARA: Not perfect, but generally OK.
GREG: I'll bet the food was great.
BARBARA: Amazing!

D UNDERSTANDING MEANING FROM CONTEXT. Use the conversation to help you choose the correct answer.

1. When Greg asks, "When did you get back?" he means _____.
   a. When did you come home?
   b. When did you go on your trip?
2. When Barbara says, "It was incredible," she means _____.
   a. It was a good trip.
   b. It wasn't a good trip.
3. When Greg says, "Good weather?" he means _____.
   a. The weather was good.
   b. Was the weather good?

WHAT ABOUT YOU?

Answer the questions about your vacations. Check all that apply.

TRAVEL SURVEY

Where do you usually go on vacation?

- ☐ I visit family.
- ☐ I go to another city.
- ☐ I go to another country.
- ☐ I go to a beach.
- ☐ Other ____________

What do you usually do on vacation?

- ☐ I take it easy.
- ☐ I visit museums and go sightseeing.
- ☐ I do a lot of physical activities.
- ☐ I eat at nice restaurants.
- ☐ Other ____________

LESSON 1

Greet Someone Arriving from a Trip

CONVERSATION MODEL Read and listen.

A: So, how was the flight?
B: Pretty nice, actually.
A: That's good. Let me help you with your things.
B: That's OK. I'm fine.

Rhythm and intonation practice

GRAMMAR. The past tense of be

Statements

The weather **was** great.
The fruits and vegetables **were** delicious.
There **was** a terrific restaurant in the hotel.
There **weren't** any problems on the flight.

I / He / She / It	was	We / You / They	were	Contractions
				wasn't = was not
				weren't = were not

Yes / no questions

Was your flight on time?
Were there any good restaurants?

Short answers

Yes, it was. / No, it wasn't.
Yes, there were. / No, there weren't.

Information questions

How was the cruise?
How long was your trip?
How many hours was the flight?

PAGES G15–G16
For more . . .

B Complete the conversations with the past tense of be.

1. **A:** Did you just get in?
   B: Yes. My flight ________ a little late.
   A: Well, how ________ your vacation?
   B: It was really incredible.

2. **A:** Welcome back! How ________ the drive?
   B: OK. But there ________ a lot of traffic.
   A: Too bad. ________ you alone?
   B: No. My brother ________ with me.

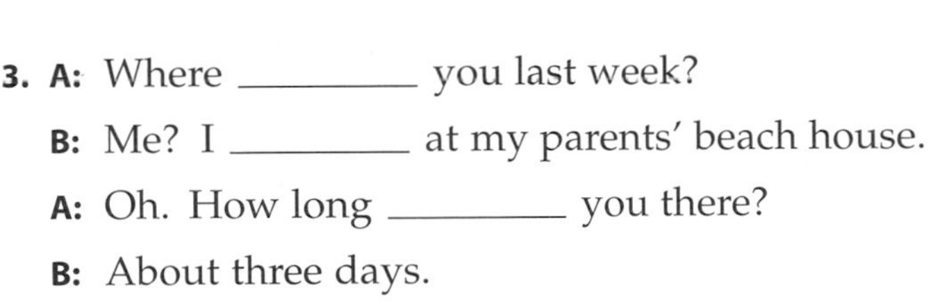

3. **A:** Where ________ you last week?
   B: Me? I ________ at my parents' beach house.
   A: Oh. How long ________ you there?
   B: About three days.

4. **A:** So, how ________ your parents' trip?
   B: It ________ terrible. They ________ so angry.
   A: ________ their train on time?
   B: No, it ________. It ________ very late.

C VOCABULARY. Adjectives for travel conditions. Listen and practice.

It was pretty **comfortable**.

It was pretty **scenic**.

It was pretty **boring**.

It was pretty **bumpy**.

It was pretty **scary**.

It was pretty **short / long**.

CONVERSATION PAIR WORK

Practice greeting someone arriving from a flight, drive, cruise, train or bus trip. Use the guide, or create a new conversation.

A: So, how was the ________?
B: Pretty ________, actually.
A: That's _____! Let me help you with your things.
B: _____.

CONTROLLED PRACTICE

LESSON 2

Talk about How You Spent Your Free Time

CONVERSATION MODEL Read and listen.

A: What did you do last weekend?
B: Nothing special. What about you?
A: Well, I went to the beach.
B: How was that?
A: I had a really nice time.

Rhythm and intonation practice

A GRAMMAR. The simple past tense

I / You / He / She / We / They **studied.**	I / You / He / She / We / They **didn't play** tennis.

Did you **have** a good time? Yes, I did. / No, I didn't.
Where **did** you **go**? I went to the beach.
When **did** they **arrive**? On Tuesday.
What **did** he **do** every day? He slept until noon.

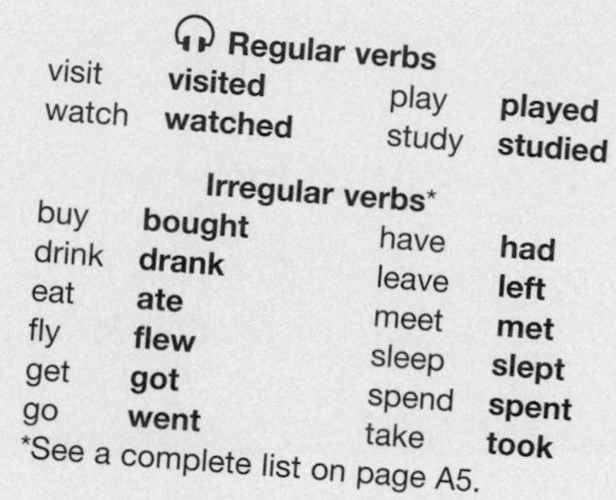

Regular verbs

visit	**visited**	play	**played**
watch	**watched**	study	**studied**

Irregular verbs*

buy	**bought**	have	**had**
drink	**drank**	leave	**left**
eat	**ate**	meet	**met**
fly	**flew**	sleep	**slept**
get	**got**	spend	**spent**
go	**went**	take	**took**

*See a complete list on page A5.

PAGES G16–G17
For more . . .

B Complete the sentences with the simple past tense.

Dear Vicky,
We're here! The flight was fine. I ______ (1. sleep) the whole time. Yesterday, we ______ (2. go) swimming. We ______ (3. eat) fresh seafood and ______ (4. drink) coconut milk from coconuts right off the trees. In the evening we ______ (5. have) a wonderful dinner. After the meal, a jazz ensemble ______ (6. play) for several hours and we ______ (7. meet) some very nice people. We ______ (8. leave (not)) until after midnight. We ______ (9. have) such a good time! This morning we ______ (10. walk) into town and ______ (11. buy) postcards. More later! Carol

Vicky Bower
22 High Street
Belleville, NY 10514
USA

LUFTPOST
PAR AVION VIA AEREA

C **Complete each question with the simple past tense.**

1. **A:** Where did you go last weekend? **B:** We went to the beach.
2. **A:** ________ you ________ a good flight? **B:** Not really. It was pretty scary.
3. **A:** ________ you ________ in the evening? **B:** We listened to music.
4. **A:** ________ you ________ at the hotel? **B:** We arrived last Monday.
5. **A:** ________ you ________ lots of souvenirs? **B:** Yes. We bought some beautiful maps.

D **PRONUNCIATION.** **The simple past tense. There are three different pronunciations of the simple past tense ending -ed. Read and listen. Then repeat.**

/d/	/t/	/ɪd/
play**ed**	watch**ed**	visit**ed**
rain**ed**	cook**ed**	need**ed**
call**ed**	stopp**ed**	wait**ed**

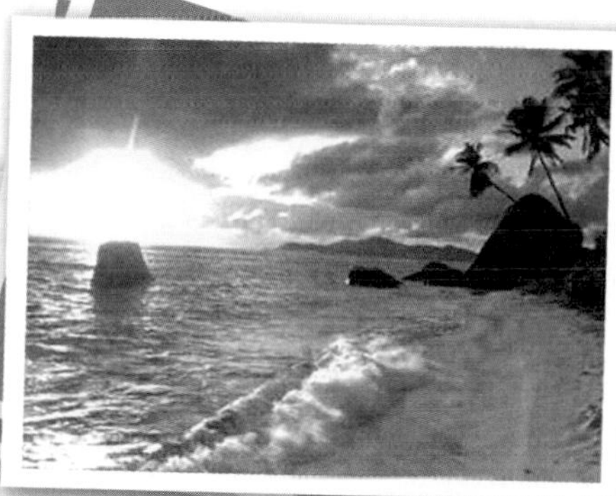

CONVERSATION PAIR WORK

Talk about how you spent your free time. Use the past time expressions.

A: What did you do ______?
B: ______ . . .

Continue the conversation, using real information or the pictures.

Past time expressions
- last weekend
- last week
- last night
- yesterday
- over the summer
- on your vacation

the zoo

a baseball game

a movie

a museum

LESSON 3

Discuss Vacation Preferences

A **VOCABULARY.** **Adjectives to describe a vacation. Listen and practice.**

It was so **relaxing**.

It was so **exciting**.

It was so **interesting**.

It was so **unusual**.

B **READING WARM-UP.** **Describe your dream vacation.**

C **READING.** **Read the vacation ads. Then use one or more adjectives from the vocabulary for each vacation.**

TOP NOTCH TRAVEL *has your dream vacation!*

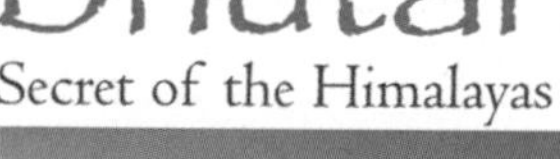

"Everyone was happy to practice their English and walk with us."

There are many beautiful places on this earth, but Bhutan is unique. Few tourists go there, but you can be one of them. View scenic mountains and meet friendly people dressed in traditional clothing.

www.countrywalkers.com

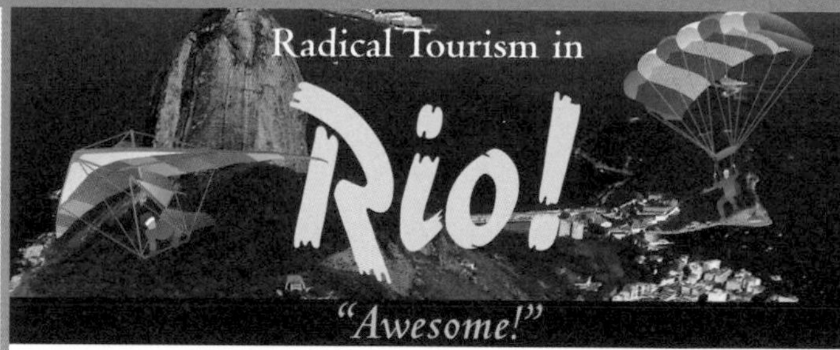

Are you looking for EXTREME ADVENTURE? How about skydiving or hang gliding over Rio? Jump with us from a plane flying at over 4,000 meters. Or fly slowly like a bird over the famous white sand beaches and mountains of Rio. As close as it gets to heaven you won't want to come down! No experience required!

www.rioadventuretours.com

EUROPEAN LANGUAGE TOUR

Enjoy Europe, Learn a Language!

"I had a great time and I learned so much!"

Attend classes three to four hours a day and have the afternoon free for sightseeing. Stay with a local family—and practice your new language. Study French, Italian, Greek, and more! Classes available for all levels.

www.europeforvisitors.com

sea mountain

inn and spa

"What an experience!"

The best of Southern California! Enjoy our scenic Pacific Ocean views. Walk through our Asian gardens and swim in our beautiful pool. Work out in our gym with weights, running machines, or stationary bikes. Eat our delicious and healthful meals and relax with a soothing massage.

www.seamountain.com

 **PAIR WORK.** **Choose a vacation for each person. Use the ads on page 94. Discuss your answers.**

"I work hard all year. I need a vacation where someone will take care of me."

"I love to meet people and learn about new cultures. I'm over fifty, but I like to learn new things."

"I'm an athlete and I love sports. I always like to do something new and different."

"I like to go to places where other people don't go—'off the beaten path.'"

 **WHAT ABOUT YOU?** **Choose a vacation for yourself.**

TOP NOTCH INTERACTION

Do You Need a Vacation?

STEP 1. Take the vacation survey. Then compare your answers with a partner.

What's important to you in a vacation? Check ☑ all that apply.

I like

- ❑ exciting vacations
- ❑ relaxing vacations
- ❑ interesting vacations
- ❑ unusual vacations
- ❑ inexpensive vacations
- ❑ _________ vacations

I like vacations with

- ❑ lots of history and culture
- ❑ lots of nature and wildlife
- ❑ lots of sports or physical activities
- ❑ lots of family activities
- ❑ lots of entertainment
- ❑ people who speak my language
- ❑ beautiful hotels
- ❑ great food
- ❑ warm weather
- ❑ nice beaches
- ❑ friendly people
- ❑ _________

STEP 2. GROUP WORK. Discuss vacation preferences with your classmates. Use your survey for support.

- What's important to you in a vacation?
- How often do you go on vacation?
- Do you need a vacation right now? Why?

LESSON

Tell about Your Experiences on a Trip

A **VOCABULARY. Problems during a trip. Listen and practice.**

The weather **was terrible**.

The people **were unfriendly**.

They canceled my flight.

Someone stole my wallet.

B **LISTENING COMPREHENSION. Listen to the conversations about vacations and check ☑ all the statements that are true. Then listen again and check your work.**

1. ☐ Someone stole her car. ☐ Someone stole her wallet. ☐ They canceled her flight.
2. ☐ They canceled her flight. ☐ They canceled her reservation. ☐ The people were unfriendly.
3. ☐ They canceled her flight. ☐ The people were unfriendly. ☐ Her vacation was too short.

C **Look at the pictures. Write about the problems.**

1. The food was terrible.

2. The waiters ______________.

3. ______________ my hotel reservation.

4. ______________ my purse.

5. The entertainment ______________.

6. ______________ my luggage.

TOP NOTCH
INTERACTION • *How Was Your Vacation?*

STEP 1. Read two articles students wrote about their vacations.

In 2002, I went on vacation to Hawaii. It was very relaxing and the weather was perfect. On the other hand there were some problems. Our hotel wasn't very good. Also, the food was terrible and the waiters and waitresses were unfriendly.

Last summer, I visited my brother for a week. I took a train and the trip was very scenic. That week, we did a lot of exciting things together. We went horseback riding in the mountains, and we went swimming in the ocean. I also learned how to play golf.

STEP 2. On the notepad, write notes about a vacation you took.

place: ____ transportation: ____

weather: ____ food / service / hotel / people: ____

activities: ____

STEP 3. PAIR WORK. Ask about your partner's vacation. Then tell the class about your partner's vacation.

NEED HELP? **Here's language you already know:**

Ask

How was [the weather]?
What did you do in [the evening]?
Tell me something about ____.
What was wrong with [the food]?
That's [great].
I'm sorry to hear that.
What do you mean?
I'd love to go to ____.

Describe

What do you want to know?
We had a ____ time.
We usually ____.
Sometimes we ____.
The [flight] was [long].
The [beach] was [relaxing].
The [people] were [friendly].

Complain

[The bus driver] drove me crazy!
The ____ didn't work.
The ____ was clogged.
I was in the mood for ____, but …
They didn't accept ____.
The dress code was ____.

STEP 4. WRITING. Write about your vacation. Use your notepad for support.

UNIT 8 CHECKPOINT

A LISTENING COMPREHENSION. Listen critically to people talking about their travel experiences. Then listen again to complete the sentences. Circle the letter of the best answer.

1. It was very ____. a. short b. scary c. scenic
2. It was very ____. a. scary b. unusual c. relaxing
3. It was very ____. a. short b. scary c. scenic
4. It was very ____. a. short b. scenic c. boring

B Complete each sentence or question. Use the past tense form.

1. I ________ (buy) a lot of souvenirs on my vacation.
2. Where ________ you ________ (eat) dinner every night?
3. We ________ (sleep) right on the beach. It ________ (be) so relaxing.
4. My sister ________ (get) back last weekend. She ________ (have) a great time.
5. My friend ________ (eat) a lot of good food on her trip to Hong Kong.
6. When ________ she ________ (arrive) at the hotel?
7. I had a terrible time. The people ________ (be) very unfriendly.
8. We ________ (see) an excellent play in London. And it ________ (be) very inexpensive.
9. My wife and I ________ (go) running every morning on the beach.
10. My brother says he ________ (meet) a lot of friendly people on his trip.

C Complete each conversation with a question in the simple past tense.

1. **A:** ______________________ on vacation?
   B: We went to Spain.
2. **A:** ______________________ every evening?
   B: We watched TV and read books.
3. **A:** ______________________ get back home?
   B: Last night.

***TOP NOTCH* SONG**
"My Dream Vacation"
Lyrics on last page before Workbook.

***TOP NOTCH* PROJECT**
Bring in travel ads. In a small group, choose a vacation. Tell the class about it.

***TOP NOTCH* WEBSITE**
For Unit 8 online activities, visit the *Top Notch* Companion Website at www.longman.com/topnotch.

Unit Wrap-Up

- **Social language.** Create conversations for the people.
  How was your vacation?
- **Grammar.** Talk about the woman's vacation. Use the past tense.
- **Writing.** Write a story about her vacation.
  The flight was very bumpy ...

Now I can ...

- ☐ greet someone arriving from a trip.
- ☐ talk about how I spent my free time.
- ☐ discuss vacation preferences.
- ☐ tell about my experiences on a trip.

UNIT 9

Taking Transportation

UNIT GOALS

1 Discuss schedules and buy tickets
2 Book travel services
3 Understand airport announcements
4 Describe transportation problems

A TOPIC PREVIEW. **Look carefully at the departure schedule and the clock. What time is the next flight to São Paulo?**

RAPID AIR BRASILIA DEPARTURES

Destination	FLT/No.	Departs	Gate	Status
São Paulo	56	15:50	G4	departed
Belo Horizonte	267	16:10	G3	boarding
Rio de Janeiro	89	16:10	G9	boarding
São Paulo	58	16:50	G4	now 17:25
São Luis	902	17:00	G3	on time
São Paulo	60	17:50	G4	delayed
Porto Alegre	763	17:50	G3	on time
Caracas	04	18:05	G1	canceled
Rio de Janeiro	91	18:10	G9	on time
São Paulo	62	18:50	G4	on time

B DISCUSSION. **How often do you fly? Complete the chart with flights you took or that someone you know took. Tell your class about them.**

"My mom went to Cheju in 2002. She took Asiana."

Destination	Year	Airline
Cheju, Korea	2002	Asiana

C 🎧 **SOUND BITES. Read along silently as you listen to a natural conversation.**

MARMO: Excuse me. Do you speak English?

ROBERT: Yes. But actually I'm French.

MARMO: I'm looking for the bullet train.

ROBERT: Which one?

MARMO: The Nozomi. To Kyoto. Leaving at 10:20.

ROBERT: I'm taking that, too. You can follow me. It leaves from track 15.

MARMO: Thanks. But we should hurry. It's going to leave in seven minutes.

ROBERT: By the way, where are you from?

MARMO: Jakarta. I'm Indonesian.

ROBERT: No kidding! I'm going to Indonesia next week.

MARMO: Really? What a small world!

D **Read the statements critically. Check ☑ the statements that you are sure are true.**

☐ **1.** The Nozomi is a bullet train.

☐ **2.** Both travelers are taking the bullet train.

☐ **3.** The train is going to leave soon.

☐ **4.** Robert goes to Indonesia often.

WHAT ABOUT **YOU?**

What are your travel plans?

TRAVEL SURVEY

Where are you going to travel in the next few years?

☐ Asia ☐ Africa ☐ Europe
☐ North America ☐ South America ☐ Other ______

What means of transportation are you going to take?

☐ Airplane ☐ Ship ☐ Car
☐ Train ☐ Bus ☐ Other ______

What language(s) are you going to speak on your trip?

☐ My native language ☐ English ☐ Other ______

LESSON 1

Discuss Schedules and Buy Tickets

CONVERSATION MODEL Read and listen.

A: Can we make the 2:00 bus to Puebla?
B: No, I'm sorry. It left five minutes ago.
A: Oh, no! What should we do?
B: Well, you could take the 2:30.
A: OK. Two tickets, please.
B: One way or round trip?
A: Round trip.

Rhythm and intonation practice

A **VOCABULARY.** **Tickets and trips. Listen and practice.**

PASSENGER TICKET
KOREA BUS LINE
SEOUL > SOKCHO

a one-way ticket

PASSENGER TICKET
KOREA BUS LINE
SEOUL > SOKCHO
SOKCHO > SEOUL

a round-trip ticket

JAPAN RAIL	Kodama (local)	Nozomi (express)
Tokyo	10:13	10:20
Odawara	10:30	–
Atami	11:00	–
Maibara	13:39	–
Kyoto	14:04	12:38

a local **an express**

a direct flight

a non-stop flight

an aisle seat **a window seat**

B **Complete the conversations with appropriate words and phrases from the vocabulary.**

1. **A:** Would you like a window or an aisle?
   B: ________. I need to stretch my legs.
2. **A:** Is Flight 009 a ________ flight?
   B: No. It's a ________ flight. It makes two stops, but you don't have to change planes.
3. **A:** Do you want a ________ ticket?
   B: Actually, I need a one-way ticket.
4. **A:** I'm sorry. You missed the express.
   B: Oh, no! Well, can I still make the ________?
5. **A:** Do you want the window or the aisle?
   B: I'd like the ________, please. I hear the mountains are beautiful.

C GRAMMAR. could and should

could

Use could and the base form of a verb to suggest an alternative or a possibility.

The express bus is full. You **could take** the local instead.

should

Use should and the base form of a verb to give advice.

You **shouldn't take** that flight. You **should take** the non-stop.

Questions

Could I **take** the 2:20? — Yes, you **could**. / No, you **couldn't**.

Who **should get** the aisle seat? — I **should**. I like to walk around.

PAGES G17–G18
For more . . .

D Complete each sentence or question with should or could and the base form of the verb.

1. When ____________ (we / leave) for the airport? There's going to be a lot of traffic.
2. ____________ (They / not take) the local bus. It makes too many stops.
3. You have two options. ____________ (You / take) the express bus or ____________ (you / fly).
4. That train's always crowded. ____________ (He / get) his ticket in advance.
5. ____________ (He / buy) it at a travel agency, but it's cheaper on the Internet.
6. Tell her ____________ (she / choose) the direct flight. It's better than changing planes.

CONVERSATION PAIR WORK

Discuss schedules and tickets. Use the train departure board and the clock. Use the guide, or create a new conversation.

A: Can I make the _____ to _____?
B: No, I'm sorry. It left _____ ago.
A: _____! What should I do?
B: Well, you could take the _____.
A: _____ . . .

Continue the conversation any way you like.

DEPARTURES 7:26 A.M.

To	Departs	Track
Washington	7:10	6
Boston	7:22	9
Philadelphia	7:25	19
Washington	8:25	8
Boston	8:26	24
Philadelphia	8:31	18

LESSON

2 Book Travel Services

CONVERSATION MODEL Read and listen.

A: I'm going to need a rental car in Dubai.
B: Certainly. What date are you arriving?
A: April 6th.
B: What time do you get in?
A: Let me check . . . 5:45.

Rhythm and intonation practice

VOCABULARY. Travel services. Listen and practice.

a rental car

a taxi

a limousine

a hotel reservation

B LISTENING COMPREHENSION. Listen to the conversations about travel services. Then listen again and write the service each client needs. Listen again if necessary to check your work.

1. ______________________
2. ______________________
3. ______________________
4. ______________________

GRAMMAR. Be going to for the future

Use be going to + the base form of a verb to talk about the future.

be	going to	base form
I'm	going to	**rent** a car in New York.
She's	going to	**be** at the airport.
We're	going to	**take** a taxi into town.

Are they going to get a round-trip ticket?	Yes, they are. / No, they aren't.
Who's going to make the reservation?	We are.
When are you going to call?	At 8:00.

Remember: The present continuous and the simple present tense can also express future actions.
We'**re flying** to Madrid. The plane **leaves** at 6:00.

PAGES G18–G19
For more . . .

D **Complete each sentence or question with be going to and the base form of the verb.**

1. ________ (they / buy) tickets for the express.
2. When ________ (she / call) the travel agent?
3. ________ (we / reserve) seats for everyone or just for us?
4. Who ________ (meet) him at the airport?

E **Complete the e-mail. Circle the correct forms.**

Here's my travel information: I (1. leaving / 'm leaving) Mexico City at 4:45 P.M. on Atlas Airlines flight 6702. The flight (2. arriving / arrives) in Chicago at 9:50 P.M. Mara's flight (3. be going to get in / is getting in) ten minutes later, so we (4. 're meeting / meeting) at the baggage claim. That's too late for you to pick me up, so I (5. 'm going to take / taking) a limo from O'Hare. Mara (6. goes to / is going to) come along and (7. spend / spending) the night with us. Her flight to Tokyo (8. not leaving / doesn't leave) until the next day.

CONVERSATION PAIR WORK

Book a rental car, taxi, limousine, or hotel. Use the tickets for arrival information. Use the guide, or create a new conversation.

BOARDING PASS
EXCELA RAIL TRANSPORT
JUNE 26 EXPRESS TRAIN
NEW YORK TO WASHINGTON
DEPARTURE: 6:00PM
ARRIVAL: 9:10 PM

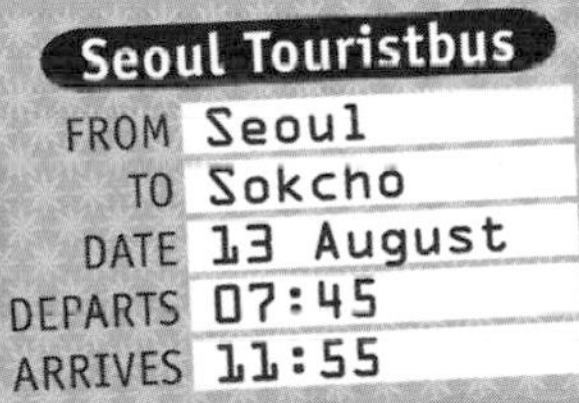

A: I'm going to need _____ in _____.
B: _____. What date are you arriving?
A: _____.
B: What time does the _____ arrive?
A: Let me check.... _____.
B: _____...

Continue the conversation in your own way ...

LESSON 3

Understand Airport Announcements

A **VOCABULARY.** **Airline passenger information. Listen and practice.**

a passenger | an agent
a boarding pass

security

an overbooking

a cancellation

B **LISTENING COMPREHENSION.** **Listen to the airport announcements and check ☑ the problems that are announced.**

- ☐ a delay
- ☐ a cancellation
- ☐ an overbooking
- ☐ a gate change
- ☐ a security problem
- ☐ a mechanical problem

C **Now listen again and write the flight information.**

1. flight number: _____
2. original departure gate: _____
3. final departure gate: _____
4. final departure time: _____

D **PRONUNCIATION.** **Stating alternatives. Listen to the rhythm and intonation of alternatives. Then listen again and repeat.**

- Well, you could take the train, or take the bus.
- They could wait or reserve a later flight.
- Would you like a one-way ticket or a round-trip ticket?

Antofagasta, Chile

TOP NOTCH
INTERACTION • *Overbooked!*

STEP 1. Read the announcement by the gate agent for Rapid Air flight 58 from Brasilia to São Paulo.

STEP 2. PAIR WORK. You and your partner have tickets on Flight 58. Read the facts.

- The time is now 16:35.
- You have a very important dinner in São Paulo at 20:30.
- The flight takes two hours.

Now look at the departure schedule and discuss your alternatives.

DEPARTURES

São Paulo	56	16:20	departed
Rio de Janeiro	89	16:40	boarding
São Paulo	58	16:50	now 17:25
São Paulo	60	17:50	on time

NEED HELP? **Here's language you already know:**

Discuss plans

What are you going to do?
What should we do?
You could ____.
We should ____.
What about ____?
Can we make the ____?
It departed ____ ago.
What time does ____ arrive?
Is it direct / non-stop?
I'm going to ____.

STEP 3. DISCUSSION. Tell the class what you decided and why. How many students decided to take a later flight?

LESSON

Describe Transportation Problems

A VOCABULARY. **Transportation problems. Listen and practice.**

We **had an accident**.

We **had mechanical problems**.

We **missed our train**.

We **got bumped** from the flight.

We **got seasick**.

B LISTENING COMPREHENSION. **Listen to the conversations. Then listen again and complete each statement with a phrase from the vocabulary.**

1. They got ________.
2. They had ________.
3. They got ________.
4. They had ________.
5. They missed ________.

C READING WARM-UP. **Do your trips always go well?**

D READING. **Read the news clippings. Which clipping is the most interesting? Explain your opinion.**

Runaway train travels 70 miles

A train from the CSX Company left Stanley Yard today when the engineer accidentally hit the power lever instead of the brake. The train was caught 70 miles later, near Toledo, Ohio. There were no injuries.

MYSTERY CRUISE SHIP ILLNESSES END

Incidents of sickness are now over, according to a cruise industry spokesperson. He was referring to numerous outbreaks of illness on cruises in recent weeks.

Dave Forney of the Centers for Disease Control and Prevention agrees. Poor sanitation in handling food was probably responsible for the recent outbreaks. "It's always important to wash hands and prepare food safely," adds Forney.

TURKEYS ENTER COCKPIT

On March 9, a small plane operated by Atlantic Coast Airlines was en route from Dulles International Airport near Washington to LaGuardia Airport in New York, when the aircraft was struck by two wild turkeys. There were four crew members and fifty passengers on board. The pilot reported that the turkeys entered the cockpit through the pilot's window. No one was injured.

SOURCES: cnn.com and ntsb.gov

E **Complete each statement to predict what each person probably said.**

1. The train engineer probably said, "_____."
   a. I almost had an accident. **b.** I almost missed the train.
2. The cruise industry spokesperson probably said, "_____."
   a. The passengers ate bad food. **b.** The passengers got seasick.
3. The pilot of the plane probably said, "_____."
   a. We had mechanical problems. **b.** We almost had an accident.

TOP NOTCH
INTERACTION • *Travel Woes*

STEP 1. Circle all the transportation you have taken. Then add other transportation you have taken.

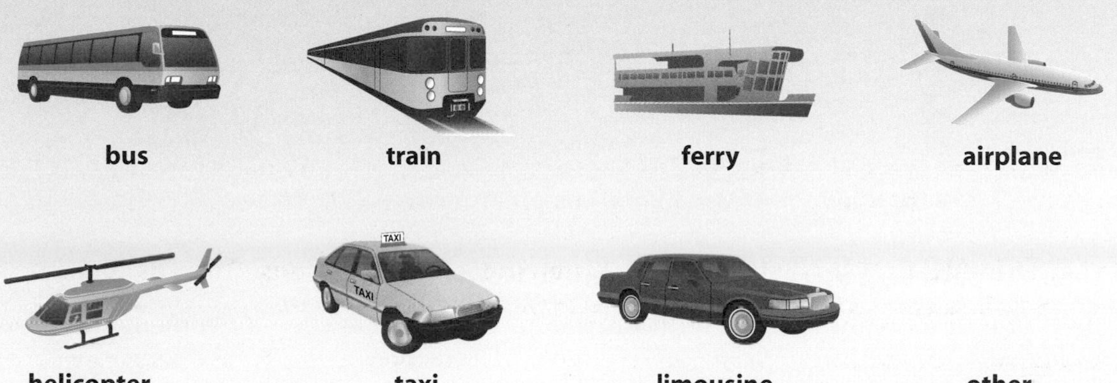

bus **train** **ferry** **airplane**

helicopter **taxi** **limousine** **other** ______

STEP 2. Ask your partner questions about the transportation he or she circled.

" When was the last time you took a train? "

STEP 3. Choose a trip when you had transportation problems. On the notepad, make notes about the trip.

means of transportation:

when:

destination:

good memories:

problems:

STEP 4. GROUP WORK. Tell your story to the class. Ask your classmates questions about their trips.

STEP 5. WRITING. Write the true story of what happened. Use your notepad for support.

Last summer I went to Tanzania. I traveled from Dar es Salaam to Songea. The bus was very comfortable and not expensive. It had air-conditioning and a bathroom. But I always get bus sick, so ...

UNIT 9
CHECKPOINT

A LISTENING COMPREHENSION. **Listen to the conversations. Then listen again and write the number of the conversation below each picture.**

_____ _____ 1 _____ _____

B **Complete each sentence with an appropriate word or phrase.**

1. If you don't want to drive to the airport, a ________ is very convenient and practical.
2. A ________ is a large car with a driver.
3. If you are not returning, you should buy a ________ ticket.
4. A ________ flight is faster than a direct flight.
5. In order to board a plane, you have to give a ________ to the agent at the gate.

C **Write an answer to each statement.**

1. "Can we still make the 6:00 ferry?" YOU ________________________________.
2. "Why are you buying a one-way ticket?" YOU ________________________________.
3. "Oh, no! When did it leave?" YOU ________________________________.

D **Complete the conversation with be going to and the indicated verbs.**

A: On Saturday, ______________ (1. we / leave) for Cancun.

B: Really? ______________ (2. you / rent) a car there? There are some great places to explore.

A: No. I think ______________ (3. we / stay) on the beach and rest. By the way, where ______________ (4. you and Margo / go) for your vacation?

B: I'm not sure. But ______________ (5. I / travel) to Bangkok on business next month. And ______________ (6. I / take) a few days off to go sightseeing. I hear it's great.

E WRITING. **On a separate sheet of paper, write a paragraph about your next trip. Use the questions for support.**

- Where are you going to go?
- What kind of transportation are you going to take?
- When do you leave?
- Who are you traveling with?
- What are you going to do when you are there?
- When do you get back?

***TOP NOTCH* PROJECT**
Use the Internet to plan travel arrangements. Use real schedules and travel services.

***TOP NOTCH* WEBSITE**
For Unit 9 online activities, visit the *Top Notch* Companion Website at www.longman.com/topnotch.

UNIT WRAP-UP

- **Social language.** Choose one picture. Create a conversation for the people. Use could and should.
- **Writing.** Tell the story in the pictures. Use the times and dates.

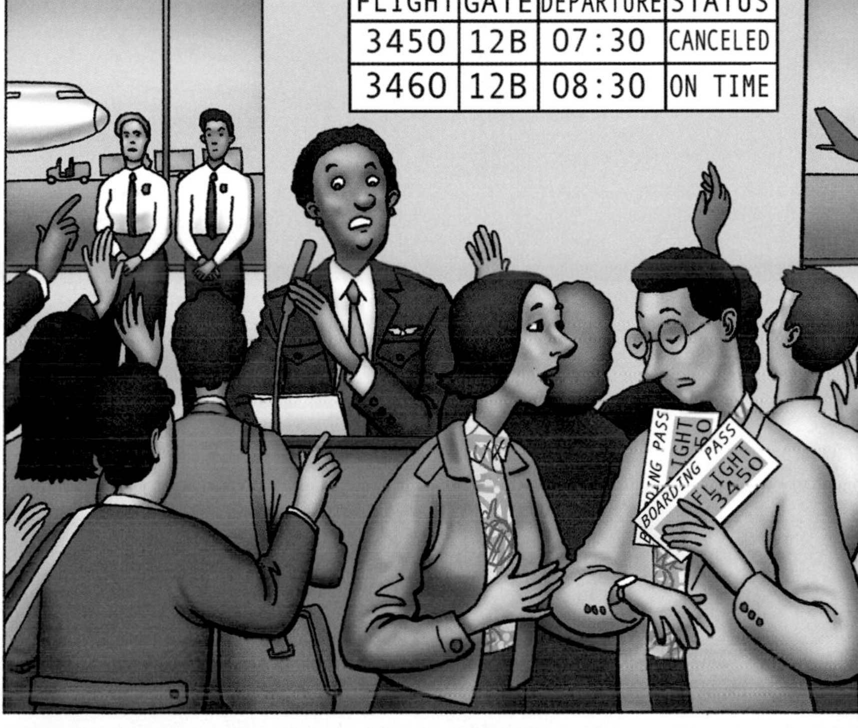

Now I can ...

- ☐ discuss schedules and buy tickets.
- ☐ book travel services.
- ☐ understand airport announcements.
- ☐ describe transportation problems.

UNIT 10

Shopping Smart

UNIT GOALS

1 Ask for a recommendation
2 Bargain for a lower price
3 Discuss tipping customs
4 Talk about a shopping experience

TOPIC PREVIEW. Look at the information in the travel guide for Toronto. Do you ever use traveler's checks, credit cards, or ATMs?

When you're in TORONTO ...

TRAVELER'S CHECKS ▶
The easiest and safest way to carry money in Canada is in traveler's checks.

▼ CREDIT CARDS
You can use credit cards at most stores and restaurants. However, some smaller businesses don't accept them. Make sure you always carry some cash.

◀ CHANGING MONEY
Banks usually offer the best exchange rates. Remember to bring your passport.

ATMs ▶
Get cash 24 hours a day from ATMs (called *bank machines* in Canada) at banks, bus and train stations, and large supermarkets.

▲ TIPPING
Leave a tip of about 10–15% of a restaurant bill or taxi fare. Restaurant bills for larger groups may include a service charge. Also tip hairdressers and hotel staff.

BARGAINING ▶
While shopping in Toronto, it's generally not the custom to bargain for a lower price.

SOURCE: based on information from www.roughguides.com

B DISCUSSION. How do you pay for things when you travel? Do you usually bargain for a lower price when you go shopping? Where is it OK to bargain? Are you a good bargainer?

C SOUND BITES. Read along silently as you listen to a natural conversation.

KAY: Oh, no. I'm almost out of cash. And I'm looking for a gift for my mother.

AMY: That's OK. I'm sure these shops accept credit cards. Let's go in here. They have really nice stuff.

KAY: Good idea.

AMY: What about this?

KAY: It's gorgeous, but it's a bit more than I want to spend.

AMY: Maybe you could get a better price.

KAY: You think so?

AMY: Well, it can't hurt to ask.

D UNDERSTANDING MEANING FROM CONTEXT. Choose the best answer.

1. When Kay says, "I'm almost out of cash," she means ______.
   a. I don't have much money. b. I have a lot of money.
2. When Amy says, "It can't hurt to ask," she means ______.
   a. It's a good idea to ask. b. It's not a good idea to ask.
3. When Kay says, "It's gorgeous," she means ______.
   a. It's very pretty. b. I don't really like it.
4. When Amy says, "Maybe you could get a better price," she means ______.
   a. This is a good price. b. Bargain with the salesperson.

WHAT ABOUT **YOU?**

What do you usually do when you're out of cash?

☐ I go to the bank.
☐ I use a credit card.
☐ I get money from an ATM.
☐ other __________.

LESSON

1 Ask for a Recommendation

CONVERSATION MODEL Read and listen.

A: I'm looking for a digital camera. Which is the least expensive?
B: The X80. But it's not the best. How much can you spend?
A: No more than 350.
B: Well, we've got some good ones in your price range.
A: Great. Could I have a look?

Rhythm and intonation practice

A GRAMMAR. Superlative adjectives

Irregular forms
good → better → **the best**
bad → worse → **the worst**

Use superlative adjectives to compare more than two people, places, or things.

Which camera is **the cheapest** of these three?
Which brands are **the most popular** in your store?

adjective	comparative	superlative	adjective	comparative	superlative
cheap	cheaper	**the cheapest**	comfortable	more comfortable	**the most comfortable**
nice	nicer	**the nicest**	portable	more portable	**the most portable**
easy	easier	**the easiest**	difficult	less difficult	**the least difficult**
big	bigger	**the biggest**	expensive	less expensive	**the least expensive**

PAGES G19–G20
For more . . .

B Write the superlative form of the adjective. Use the.

1. **A:** All of these cameras are easy to use.
   B: But which is ________________? (small)
2. **A:** All of our sweaters are pretty warm.
   B: But which brand makes ________________ ones? (heavy)
3. **A:** She wrote at least six books about Italy. They're pretty interesting.
   B: Which of her books is ________________? (interesting)
4. **A:** Do you want to take a taxi, bus, or train to the airport?
   B: Which is ________________? (convenient)

C VOCABULARY. Electronic products. Listen and practice.

a digital camera

a camcorder

a DVD player

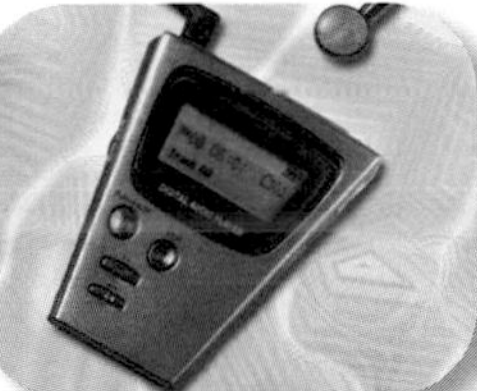
an MP3 player

a scanner

D LISTENING COMPREHENSION. Listen to the conversations at an electronics store. Then listen again and write the electronic product the people are talking about.

1. ______ 2. ______ 3. ______ 4. ______

CONVERSATION PAIR WORK

Ask for a recommendation. Use the ads, changing the prices to local currency if you wish. You can use this guide, or create a new conversation.

A: I'm looking for ____.
Which is the ____?

B: The ____. But it's not ____.
How much can you spend?

A: No more than ____.

B: ____ . . .

Continue the conversation in your <u>own</u> way . . .

Ideas
the nicest
the most popular
the lightest
the most practical
the easiest to use

LESSON

2 Bargain for a Lower Price

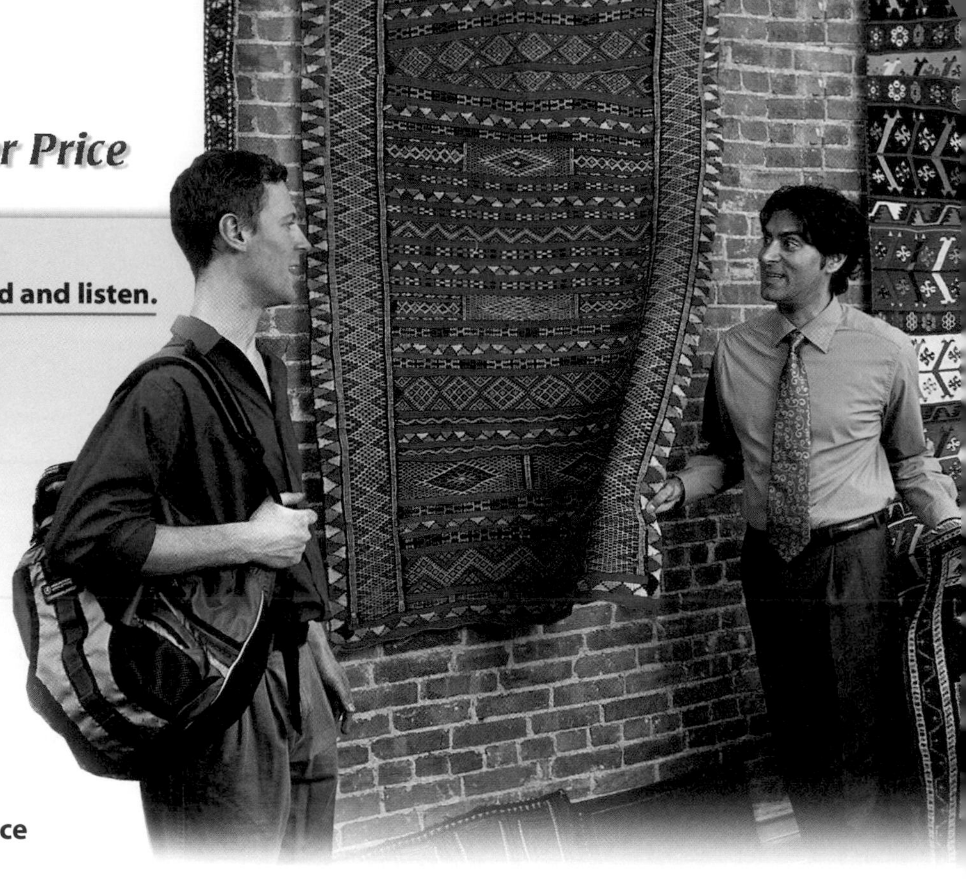

CONVERSATION MODEL Read and listen.

A: How much do you want for that rug?
B: This one?
A: No, that one's not big enough. The other one.
B: 300.
A: That's a lot more than I want to pay. I can give you 200.
B: How about 225?
A: OK. That sounds fair.

Rhythm and intonation practice

A GRAMMAR. too and enough

When something is not satisfactory:

Those rugs are **too small**.	OR	Those rugs are **not big enough**.
That camera is **too heavy**.	OR	That camera is **not light enough**.

When something is satisfactory:

This PDA is **small enough**. I'll take it.

PAGE G21
For more . . .

B Complete the conversations with the adjectives from the box. Use too or enough.

noisy	fast	expensive	small	hot	big

1. **A:** That microwave oven needs to be ________ for my family. We're very busy.
   B: Oh, yes. The X11 is our fastest model.

2. **A:** These pumps aren't ________. They're very uncomfortable.
   B: I'm so sorry. Let me get you a larger size.

3. **A:** My photocopier is ________. It's driving me crazy!
   B: Then let me show you a quieter model.

4. **A:** We ordered the hot appetizers. These aren't ________.
B: Of course, sir. I'll take care of that right away.

5. **A:** How about this pocket TV? It's pretty small.
B: That's definitely ________. Thanks.

6. **A:** This jacket is a bargain. It's only $495.
B: I'm sorry. That's just ________ for me.

C **PRONUNCIATION.** **Confirming and clarifying information. Listen to the rising intonation to confirm. Then repeat.**

A: How much is that rug?
B: This one?
A: That's right.

A: Could I have a look at that sweater?
B: The red one?
A: No, the black one.

D **VOCABULARY.** **Handicrafts. Listen and practice.**

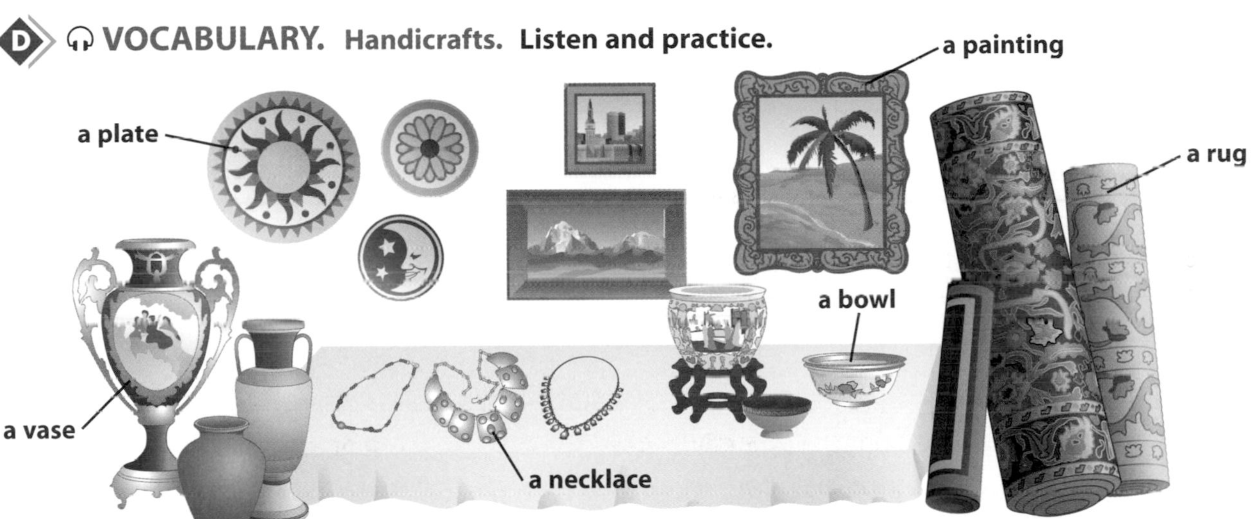

CONVERSATION PAIR WORK

With a partner, bargain for a lower price. Use the pictures above, giving a price to each item. Start like this:

A: How much do you want for that _____?
B: This one?
A: _____ . . .

Continue the conversation in your own way . . .

LESSON

3 Discuss Tipping Customs

A READING WARM-UP. Do you think tipping is a good idea or a bad idea?

B READING. Read the article about tipping customs. Is any of the information surprising to you? Explain.

Did you remember to leave a tip?

In some countries tipping is very common. In others, tipping is not expected. Here are some tipping customs from around the world.

Australia

Australians are pretty relaxed about tips—people do not usually expect them. Many people will be quite surprised if you give them a tip. Customers do leave a 10–15% tip in nicer restaurants, but don't tip taxi drivers. Instead, you can just say "Keep the change," and round off the fare.

France

A service charge is almost always included on the bill in restaurants and cafés. If you are satisfied with the service, leave an additional small tip for the server. Tip porters about 1 euro for each piece of luggage, and leave the maid who cleans your hotel room about 1 euro per day. Taxi drivers expect 10–15% of the fare. And don't forget to tip your tour guide.

US and Canada

Tip waiters and taxi drivers anywhere from 15–20% of the total bill—depending on how satisfied you are with the service. A service charge is sometimes added to a restaurant bill if there are six or more people at the table, so you don't have to leave an additional tip. At airports and hotels, porters expect about $1 per bag. In some fast-food restaurants and coffee bars, there is a cup for small tips near the cashier.

Note: In some countries, it's not customary to give tips. Before you travel, check local tipping customs to be sure.

SOURCES: *Lonely Planet*, *Rough Guide*, *Fodor's* travel guides

C Read each person's question about tipping. Then give each person advice, according to the reading.

"I'm going to Paris, France. I'm staying in a small hotel for about six days. How much should I tip the maid?"

"I'm studying English in Sydney, Australia, and I just took a taxi home. The fare is AUS$3.60. How much should I give the taxi driver?"

"I'm visiting friends in Los Angeles, in the United States. I took ten people out for dinner. The bill is US$360. How much more should I leave for the tip?"

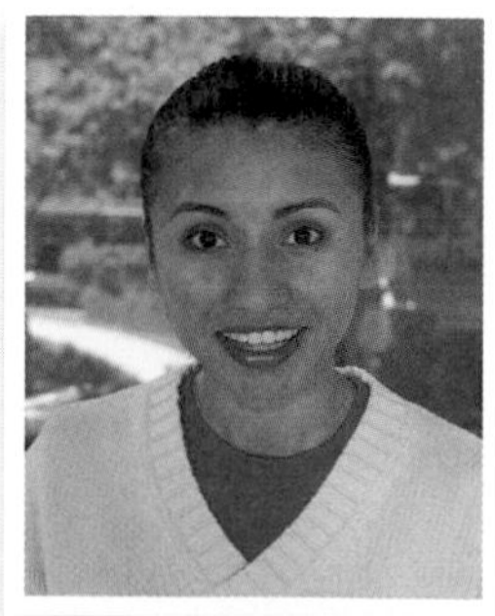

"I just arrived in Montreal, Canada, and took a taxi from the airport. The fare is CAN$6.90. How much should I tip the driver?"

TOP NOTCH
INTERACTION • *Should We Leave a Tip?*

STEP 1. What are your opinions about tipping when traveling in a country where tipping is customary? Take the opinion poll. Then compare your answers with your class.

When in Rome, do as the Romans do!

OPINION POLL

	I agree	I disagree	I'm not sure
1. Tipping is the best way to show appreciation for good service.	☐	☐	☐
2. When you're visiting another country, you should always follow its tipping customs.	☐	☐	☐
3. If the service is not good, you shouldn't tip.	☐	☐	☐
4. Restaurant bills should always include a service charge.	☐	☐	☐

STEP 2. PAIR WORK. On the notepad, write some suggestions for showing appreciation for good service in this country. If tipping is customary, explain how much to tip.

waiters / waitresses: ______________________

taxi drivers: ______________________

hotel maids: ______________________

baggage porters: ______________________

other: ______________________

STEP 3. GROUP WORK. In small groups, compare your notes. Does everyone agree?

LESSON

Talk about a Shopping Experience

A VOCABULARY. Talking about prices. Listen and practice.

She got a good price.

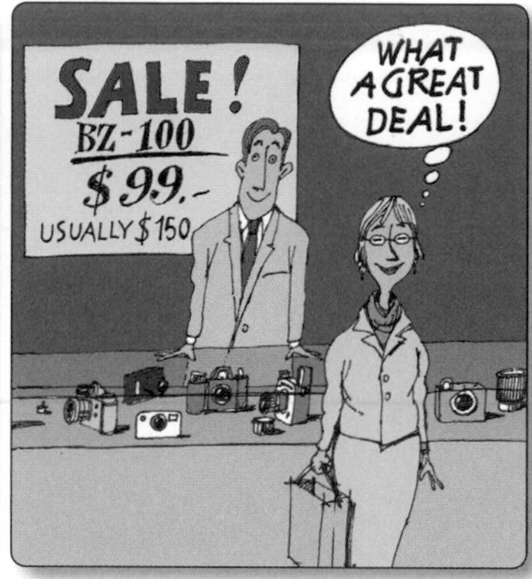

She saved a lot of money.

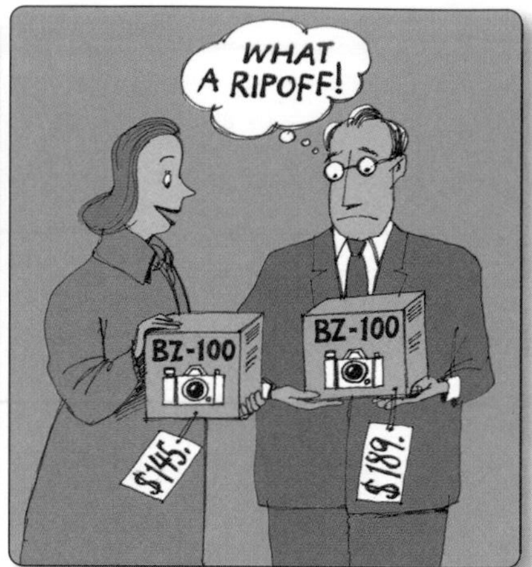

He paid too much.

NOTE: Prices can be converted to local currency if you wish.

B LISTENING COMPREHENSION. Listen to the conversations about shopping. Then listen again and complete the chart.

What did the shopper buy?	got a good price	saved a lot of money	paid too much
1. a bowl	☑	☐	☐
2.	☐	☐	☐
3.	☐	☐	☐
4.	☐	☐	☐

C DISCUSSION. Read this true story about a shopping experience. Then discuss the questions.

Several years ago, I was in Saudi Arabia on business, and I wanted to buy a small rug. I wanted to spend no more than $350 USD. I found a beautiful and unusual rug, but the asking price was too high for me: $900. The salesman and I talked about the price for a long time. Finally, he shook my hand, and I thought that was the end of the conversation.

I left the store, and he looked very surprised. Then I was surprised! He actually had agreed to my offer of $350. That's why he shook my hand. Of course, I bought the rug. What a great deal!

1. How much money did the salesman want? How much did the shopper pay?
2. Why was the shopper surprised?
3. Do you think the shopper got a good price?

TOP NOTCH
INTERACTION • *It's the Best!*

STEP 1. PAIR WORK. Discuss the questions with a partner.

1. In your own city or town, what is ...
   - the best restaurant?
   - the nicest hotel?
   - the most expensive department store?
   - the most unusual market?
   - the most interesting museum?
2. Where can you buy ...
   - the least expensive fruits and vegetables?
   - the nicest flowers?
   - the best electronics products?
   - the most unusual souvenirs?
   - the wildest clothes?

STEP 2. DISCUSSION. Discuss your choices.

"The Savoy Hotel has the biggest rooms and the best food."

"The Central Market is too expensive. The fruits and vegetables at the Old Town Market are much better and cheaper."

STEP 3. On your notepad, write notes about a good or bad shopping experience you had. Then tell the class about your experience.

What did you buy?
Where did you buy it?
How much money did the salesperson want?
Did you bargain?
How much did you pay?

STEP 4. WRITING. Write the story of your shopping experience.

UNIT **10**
CHECKPOINT

A **LISTENING COMPREHENSION.** **Listen to the conversations and write the name of the item. Then listen again critically. Check ☑ if the item is satisfactory or not satisfactory to the customer.**

	satisfactory	not satisfactory
1. *a camcorder*	☐	☑
2. ______	☐	☐
3. ______	☐	☐
4. ______	☐	☐

B **Complete the sentences.**

1. If you're out of cash, you can get money from ______.
2. If there's a service charge on the restaurant bill, you don't have to leave a ______.
3. In many countries, it's OK to ______ for a lower price.
4. You can get the best ______ at banks.
5. ______ are a safe and easy way to carry money when traveling.
6. What a ripoff. I paid ______.
7. Wow! What a great deal. I ______ a lot of money.

C **Write each sentence in another way. Use <u>too</u> or <u>enough</u>.**

1. That vase is too heavy. *That vase isn't light enough*.
2. Those cameras aren't cheap enough. ______.
3. This PDA is too big. ______.
4. These drinks aren't cold enough. ______.
5. That restaurant is too noisy. ______.

D **Write sentences about stores in your city. Use the superlative.**

Winston's Department Store has the cheapest clothing.

1. ______.
2. ______.
3. ______.
4. ______.

E **WRITING.** **On a separate sheet of paper, use your sentences to write a paragraph for a visitor to this city.**

TOP NOTCH **SONG**
"Shopping for Souvenirs"
Lyrics on last page before Workbook.

TOP NOTCH **PROJECT**
With a partner, write advice about tipping customs for a traveler to this country.

TOP NOTCH **WEBSITE**
For Unit 10 online activities, visit the *Top Notch* Companion Website at www.longman.com/topnotch.

UNIT WRAP-UP

- **Vocabulary.** Name all the things you can in the picture.
- **Social language.** Create conversations for the people.
- **Writing.** Describe what the people are doing.

Now I can ...

- ☐ ask for a recommendation.
- ☐ bargain for a lower price.
- ☐ discuss tipping customs.
- ☐ talk about a shopping experience.

Alphabetical word list for 1A and 1B

This is an alphabetical list of all productive vocabulary in the ***Top Notch 1*** units. The numbers refer to the page on which the word first appears or is defined. When a word has two meanings, both are in the list. Entries for 1A are in black. Entries for 1B are in blue.

Social language list for 1A and 1B

This is a unit-by-unit list of all the productive social language from ***Top Notch 1***.

Welcome to *Top Notch!*

Hi, my name's [Peter].
I'm [Alexandra].
Everyone calls me [Alex].
Good morning. / Good afternoon.
Good evening. / Good night.
What do you do?
I'm a [student]. And you?

[Alex], this is [Emily]. [Emily], this is [Alex].
Nice to meet you, [Emily].
Well, it was nice meeting you.
See you later.
Bye. / Good-bye.
Take it easy. / Take care.
What's this called in English?

That's right.
How do you say [your last name]?
What's your [last name], please?
I'm sorry. Could you repeat that?
Sure.
How do you spell [your first name]?
Thanks. / Thank you.

Unit 1

This is [my teacher].
Please call me [Tom].
Let me introduce you to [my wife, Carol].
Good to meet you.
Pleasure to meet you.
Are you [Bill]?

No, I'm [David].
That's [Bill] over there.
Are you [a student]?
As a matter of fact, [I am].
Is she from [São Paulo]?
Those are the [new students].
Who's that?

Come. I'll introduce you.
I'd like you to meet [Kate].
What's your name?
Where's he from?
How old are they?
Could you say that louder?

Unit 2

Do you want to see [a concert] on [Saturday]?
That's not for me.
I'm not really a [rock] fan.
What about [Sergio Mendes]?
Now that's more my style!
There's a [show] at [eleven thirty].
That's past my bedtime!
No problem.

Perfect.
See you then.
Are you free on [Friday]?
Really? (to show enthusiasm)
I'd love to go.
I'd love to go, but I'm busy on [Friday].
What time?
Too bad.
Maybe some other time.

When's the [concert]?
What time's the [movie]?
Where's the [play]?
Excuse me. (to get someone's attention)
I'm looking for [The Bell Theater].
That's right [around the corner], on the [left] side of the street.
I'm sorry, I'm not from around here.
Thanks, anyway.

Unit 3

What are you up to?
Come take a look.
Let me see.
Who's that [guy]? / Who are [those two]?
Really! (to show surprise)
Tell me something about [your family].
Sure.
What do you want to know?

Do you have any [brothers or sisters]?
I have [one younger sister].
Do they look like you?
Not really.
So what does [your sister] do?
That's great!
How about [your brother]?
How many [children] do you have?
How are you alike?

How are you different?
Do you look alike?
We wear similar clothes.
Do you both [like basketball]?
She [likes basketball], and I do too.
She doesn't [like fish], and I don't either.
He [likes coffee], but I don't.

Unit 4

This [printer] is driving me crazy!
It's not working.
It's just a lemon!
What do you mean?
What's wrong with it?
Hey, [Bob]! (as a greeting)
What are *you* doing here? (to express surprise)

I'm looking for [a laptop].
Any suggestions?
What about [a Pell]?
Really? (to ask for clarification)
How's it going?
Fine, thanks.
I'm sorry to hear that.
That's too bad. / That's a shame.

The [window] won't open / close.
The [iron] won't turn on / off.
The [fridge] is making a funny sound.
The [toilet] won't flush.
The [toilet] won't stop flushing.
The [sink] is clogged.
Hello? (to answer the telephone)
This is room [211]. Can I help you?

Unit 5

Are you ready to order?
Do you need some more time?
I think I'll start with [the soup].
Then I'll have [the chicken].
That comes with [salad], doesn't it?

There's a choice of vegetables.
Tonight we have [carrots].
Certainly.
Anything [to drink]? / And [to drink]?
What is there to [eat]?

Is that all?
I'm in the mood for [seafood].
Sorry. You're out of luck.
Let's go out!
Good idea!

I'll have the [pasta] for my [main course].
What does that come with?
What kind of [soup] is there?
I think I'll have the [salad].
What do you feel like eating [tonight]?
The [special] sounds delicious.
What about the [chicken]?
Sounds good.
Excuse me! (to get attention in a restaurant)
We're ready to order.
Would you like to start with [an appetizer]?
And for your [main course]?
We have [a nice seafood special] on the menu.
We'll take the check, please.
Is the tip included?
Do you accept credit cards?

Unit 6

Where are you off to?
I'm on my way to [the park].
Do you want to play together sometime?
That would be great.
No way.
He's a couch potato.
Too bad.
I'm crazy about [tennis].
Why don't we [play basketball] sometime?
Great idea.
When's good for you?
Sorry, I can't. (to express regret)
I have to [meet my sister at the airport].
That sounds great.
You too?
Actually, I usually go [in the evening].
How come?
Well, have a great time.
He's in shape / out of shape.
We don't eat junk food.
[They] avoid sweets.
[I have] a sweet tooth.

Unit 7

Excuse me. (to ask for assistance in a shop)
How much is that [V-neck] / are those [pants]?
That's not too bad.
Do you have it / them in [a larger size]?
It is / These are too [short].
Here you go.
Would you like to try it / them on?
No, thanks.
Would you be nice enough to [gift wrap it / them for me]?
Of course.
We have a pair in [brown].
See if they are better.
Let me see if I can find you something better.
Yes, they're fine.
I'll take the [loafers].
How would you like to pay for them?
Excuse me? (to ask for clarification)
Cash or charge?
Go straight.
Turn left / right.
Go down / up the stairs.
Take the escalator / elevator / stairs.
It's on the top / first / ground floor.
It's in the basement.
It's in the front / back.

Unit 8

When did you get back?
Just [yesterday].
Tell me about your trip.
I had a [really great] time.
I'll bet the [food] was [great].
Amazing! (to express delight)
How was the [flight]?
I was [pretty bumpy], actually.
Let me help you with your [things].
Thanks a lot.
Did you just get in?
My [flight] was [a little late].
Welcome back!
OK.
What did you do [last weekend]?
Nothing special.
What about you?
It was so [relaxing].
[The weather] was terrible.
[The people] were unfriendly.
They canceled [my flight].
Someone stole [my wallet].

Unit 9

Do you speak [English]?
I'm looking for [the bullet train].
Which one?
I'm taking that, too.
You can follow me.
It leaves from [track 15].
We should hurry.
By the way, where are you from?
No kidding!
What a small world!
Can we make the [2:00 bus]?
It left / departed [five minutes] ago.
Oh, no!
What should we do?
One way or round-trip?
I'm going to need [a rental car] in [Dubai].
What date are you arriving?
What time do you get in?
Let me check.
We had an accident / mechanical problems.
We missed our [train].
We got bumped from the flight.
We got seasick.

Unit 10

I'm almost out of cash.
Let's go in here.
What about this?
It's a bit more than I want to spend.
Maybe you could get a better price.
You think so?
It can't hurt to ask.
How much can you spend?
No more than [amount].
Could I have a look?
How much do you want for [that rug]?
This one?
The other one.
I can give you [amount].
That sounds fair.
This jacket is a bargain.
I'm sorry. That's just too much for me.
Pretty good!
What a great deal!
What a rip-off!
She got a good price.
She saved a lot of money.
He paid too much.

Pronunciation table

These are the pronunciation symbols used in *Top Notch 1*.

Vowels

Symbol	Key Words
i	beat, feed
ɪ	bit, did
eɪ	date, paid
ɛ	bet, bed
æ	bat, bad
ɑ	box, odd, father
ɔ	bought, dog
oʊ	boat, road
ʊ	book, good
u	boot, food, flu
ʌ	but, mud, mother
ə	banana, among
ɚ	shirt, murder
aɪ	bite, cry, buy, eye
aʊ	about, how
ɔɪ	voice, boy
ɪr	deer
ɛr	bare
ɑr	bar
ɔr	door
ʊr	tour

Consonants

Symbol	Key Words	Symbol	Key Words
p	pack, happy	z	zip, please, goes
b	back, rubber	ʃ	ship, machine, station, special, discussion
t	tie	ʒ	measure, vision
d	die	h	hot, who
k	came, key, quick	m	men
g	game, guest	n	sun, know, pneumonia
ʧ	church, nature, watch	ŋ	sung, ringing
ʤ	judge, general, major	w	wet, white
f	fan, photograph	l	light, long
v	van	r	right, wrong
θ	thing, breath	y	yes
ð	then, breathe		
s	sip, city, psychology		
t̬	butter, bottle		
t˺	button		

Non-count nouns

This list is an at-a-glance reference to the non-count nouns used in *Top Notch 1*.

aerobics
air-conditioning
basketball
beef
bike riding
bread
broccoli
butter
cake
candy
cash
cheese
chicken
clothing
coffee
crab
culture
dancing
dessert
dinner
electronics
English
entertainment
fish
food
fruit
golf
grain
health
history
hosiery
hot sauce
housework
ice
juice
junk food
lamb
lettuce
lingerie
meat
milk
music
nature
oil
outerwear
pasta
pepper
pie
rice
running
salad
salt
sausage
seafood
service
shopping
shrimp
sightseeing
skydiving
sleepwear
soccer
soup
squid
swimming
tennis
traffic
transportation
TV
walking
water
weather
wildlife
yogurt

Irregular verbs

base form	simple past	past participle
be	was / were	been
begin	began	begun
break	broke	broken
bring	brought	brought
build	built	built
buy	bought	bought
catch	caught	caught
choose	chose	chosen
come	came	come
cost	cost	cost
cut	cut	cut
do	did	done
drink	drank	drunk
drive	drove	driven
eat	ate	eaten
fall	fell	fallen
find	found	found
fit	fit	fit
fly	flew	flown
fall	fell	fallen
feel	felt	felt
forget	forgot	forgotten

base form	simple past	past participle
get	got	gotten
give	gave	given
go	went	gone
grow	grew	grown
have	had	had
hear	heard	heard
hit	hit	hit
hurt	hurt	hurt
keep	kept	kept
know	knew	knew
leave	left	left
lose	lost	lost
make	made	made
mean	meant	meant
meet	met	met
pay	paid	paid
put	put	put
quit	quit	quit
read	read	read
ride	rode	ridden
run	run	run
say	said	said

base form	simple past	past participle
see	saw	seen
sell	sold	sold
send	sent	sent
sing	sang	sung
sit	sat	sat
sleep	slept	slept
speak	spoke	spoken
spend	spent	spent
stand	stood	stood
steal	stole	stolen
swim	swam	swum
take	took	taken
teach	taught	taught
tell	told	told
think	thought	thought
throw	threw	thrown
understand	understood	understood
wake up	woke up	woken up
wear	wore	worn
win	won	won
write	wrote	written

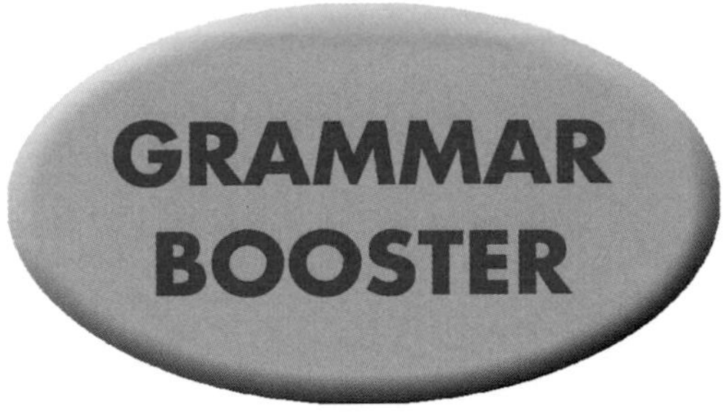

1B

GRAMMAR BOOSTER

The *Grammar Booster* is optional. It provides more explanation and practice, as well as additional grammar concepts.

UNIT 6 Lesson 1

Can: form

Use can with the base form of a verb.

She **can play** golf very well.
NOT She ~~cans play~~ golf very well.
NOT She ~~can plays~~ golf very well.
NOT She ~~can to play~~ golf very well.

There are three negative forms of can.

He **can't** swim. = He **cannot** swim. = He **can not** swim.

A **Correct the following sentences.**

1. Can you ~~coming~~ come to the party next week?
2. My brother-in-law can't plays basketball tomorrow.
3. I'm going to the pool with Diane, but I no can swim.
4. Alice can to go running after work.
5. Can Lisa visits her cousins next weekend?

Can: information questions

Where **can** I go running around here?	Try the park.
When **can** you **come** for dinner?	How about tomorrow night?
How often **can** you **go** running?	No more than twice a week. I'm pretty busy.
What languages **can** you **speak**?	I can speak Italian.
Who **can drive**?	I can.

B **Complete the questions, using can.**

1. **A:** _________ aerobics around here? (Where / I / do)
   B: Why don't you try Total Fitness? They have great instructors.
2. **A:** _________ English together? (When / we / study)
   B: Let's get together tomorrow night. OK?
3. **A:** We need some fresh air. _________ walking? (Where / we / go)
   B: Well, we can go over to Grant Park. It's very nice.
4. **A:** _________ golf? (How often / Larry / play)
   B: Not very often. He's starting a new job.
5. **A:** _________ dinner tonight? (Who / make)
   B: What about Katherine? She's not doing anything.

Have to: form

Use have to or has to with the base form of a verb. Use has to for the third-person singular.

I **have to go** to class at 9:00.
She **has to go** to class at 8:00.
NOT She ~~has to goes~~ to class at 8:00.
NOT She ~~has to going~~ to class at 8:00.

 **Correct these sentences.**

1. My brother-in-law ~~have~~ has to work on the weekend.
2. Do you has to meet Mr. Green at the airport?
3. We don't have to making dinner tonight. We're going out.
4. Ms. Davis has to fills out an application for her English class.
5. Does she have to watches TV now? I'm trying to study.

Have to: information questions

What does he **have to do** Saturday morning?	He has to clean the house.
How often does she **have to work** on the weekend?	Not often.
When do they **have to go** shopping?	Tonight. The party's tomorrow.
Who **has to write** the report?	Marian.
Where do you **have to go** this morning?	To the airport.

D **Complete the questions.**

1. **A:** _______ she _______ do tomorrow?
   B: She has to go to English class.

2. **A:** _______ he _______ take the medicine?
   B: Every three hours.

3. **A:** _______ she _______ go to the park?
   B: At around eight.

4. **A:** _______ they _______ do after class?
   B: Nothing special.

5. **A:** _______ we _______ turn off the machine?
   B: Never! Don't ever turn it off.

6. **A:** _______ you _______ pick up your sister?
   B: At about two thirty.

UNIT 6 Lesson 2

The simple present tense: non-action verbs

Some verbs are non-action verbs. Most non-action verbs are not usually used in the present continuous, even when they are describing a situation that is happening right now.

I **want** a sandwich. NOT ~~I'm wanting a sandwich.~~

Some common non-action verbs:

be have know like love miss need see understand want

Some non-action verbs have action and non-action meanings.

non-action meaning	**action meaning**
I **have** two sandwiches. (possession)	I'**m having** a sandwich. (eating)
I **think** English is difficult. (opinion)	I'**m thinking** about her. (the act of thinking)

A **Write the verbs in the simple present tense or the present continuous.**

Dear Kevin,

It's 2:00 and I __________ (1. think) of you. The kids __________ (2. play) outside. I __________ (3. see) them through the window right now. They __________ (4. have) a small table and chairs and they __________ (5. have) a late lunch.

I __________ (6. want) to mail this letter before the post office closes. I __________ (7. know) you're working hard and we all __________ (8. miss) you.

Maggie

The simple present tense: frequency adverbs

Frequency adverbs generally follow forms of the verb <u>be</u> and precede all other verbs.

be	frequency adverb
I **'m**	**usually** at the pool on Saturdays.

frequency adverb	verb
I **usually**	**go** to the pool on Saturdays.

<u>Sometimes</u>, <u>usually</u>, <u>often</u>, <u>generally</u>, and <u>occasionally</u> can also go at the beginning or the end of a sentence. Don't use the other frequency adverbs there.

Sometimes I go to the pool on Sundays.
I go to the pool **often**.
NOT <u>Never I go to the pool.</u> OR <u>I go to the pool never.</u>

In negative sentences, most frequency adverbs can precede OR follow <u>don't</u> or <u>doesn't</u>.

Hank **usually** doesn't go running on the weekend.
Hank doesn't **usually** go running on the weekend.

But note that <u>always</u> CANNOT precede <u>don't</u> or <u>doesn't</u>.

I don't **always** have breakfast in the morning.
NOT I ~~always don't have~~ breakfast in the morning.

Don't use <u>never</u> with a negative verb. Use the frequency adverb <u>ever</u> with negative verbs.

I **never** eat sweets. = I **don't ever** eat sweets.
NOT I ~~don't never~~ eat sweets.

The simple present tense: time expressions

Time expressions generally go at the beginning or the end of a sentence.

I go to the pool **three times a week.** **Three times a week**, I go to the pool.

The time expression <u>a lot</u> can appear only at the end of a sentence.

I go to the pool **a lot**. NOT ~~A lot I go~~ to the pool.

some time expressions
every week
every other day
once a month
twice a year
three times a week
other expressions
once in a while
a lot

 **These sentences are not written correctly. Rewrite them correctly.**

1. She plays usually golf on Sunday.
   ______________________.
2. They go to the park hardly ever.
   ______________________.
3. I always am hungry in the afternoon.
   ______________________.
4. We once in a while have eggs for breakfast.
   ______________________.
5. Pat doesn't never exercise.
   ______________________.
6. Never I go swimming at night.
   ______________________.
7. Victor doesn't drink always coffee.
   ______________________.
8. Connie and I play twice a week tennis together.
   ______________________.
9. We go often bike riding in the afternoon.
   ______________________.
10. She is every day late for class.
   ______________________.

UNIT 7 Lesson 1

Comparative forms of adjectives

Add <u>–er</u> to one-syllable adjectives. If the adjective ends in <u>–e</u>, add <u>–r</u>.

cheap → cheap**er** loose → loose**r**

If an adjective ends consonant-vowel-consonant, double the final consonant before adding <u>–er</u>.

hot → hot**ter**

For most adjectives that end in <u>–y</u>, change the <u>y</u> to <u>i</u> and add <u>–er</u>.

pretty → prett**ier** busy → bus**ier**

To make the comparative form of most adjectives of two or more syllables, use <u>more</u> or <u>less</u>.

She's **less practical** than her sister. DVDs are **more popular** than videos.

A **Write the comparative form of the following adjectives.**

	comparative		comparative
1. tall	taller	6. casual	______
2. pretty	______	7. wild	______
3. comfortable	______	8. informal	______
4. heavy	______	9. late	______
5. light	______	10. sad	______

B **Complete each sentence with a comparative form.**

1. This purse is ______ (nice) than that one.
2. He's a ______ (good) student than she.
3. Holland is ______ (small) than Thailand.
4. Thailand is ______ (large) than Holland.
5. Women's shoes are usually ______ (expensive) than men's shoes.

UNIT 7 Lesson 2

Direct objects

The subject of a sentence performs the action of the verb, and a direct object receives the action of the verb.

subject		direct object
I	like	**this house.**
My husband	likes	**that suit.**

A **Underline the subjects in the following sentences. Circle the direct objects.**

1. We're visiting Africa this summer.
2. Many people rent cars when they travel.
3. I love Egyptian food.
4. Sanford and Mary never eat meat.
5. You can't enter school before eight o'clock.
6. Do you have the tickets?
7. Marie wants coffee with cream.

Indirect objects

When a sentence contains a direct object and prepositional phrase, you can use an indirect object to say the same thing.

prepositional phrase	indirect object
I'm buying the gloves **for her.**	I'm buying **her** the gloves.
Give the sweater **to Ben.**	Give **Ben** the sweater.

B **Rewrite each sentence, changing the prepositional phrase into an indirect object.**

1. She buys groceries for us. She buys us groceries.
2. Laura sends a check to them every month. ______.
3. At night we read stories to them. ______.
4. They serve meals to us in the dining room. ______.
5. They never give gifts to me on my birthday. ______.

C **Rewrite each sentence, changing the indirect object into a prepositional phrase.**

1. He always gives me a check when I ask. He always gives a check to me when I ask.
2. I send them the tickets and they give me a receipt. ______.
3. Michael's assistant shows him the phone messages every day after lunch.

______.

D **Add the indirect object to each sentence. Don't add words.**

to me	1. They send it on Monday. They send it to me on Monday.
you	2. Do they give breakfast on the tour? ______?
her	3. We always tell the truth. ______.
for him	4. They make extra time. ______.

UNIT 8 Lesson 1

The past tense of be: form

Use was or were for affirmative statements. Use wasn't or weren't for negative statements.

I **was** there yesterday. They **were** there, too.
She **wasn't** my teacher. They **weren't** my classmates.

The past tense of be: questions

Begin yes / no questions with Was or Were.

Was your flight on time? **Were** you late?

Begin information questions with a question word followed by was or were.

How long was the flight? **Where were** your passports?

A **Complete the conversations with was, were, wasn't, or weren't.**

1. **A:** ______ you out of town last week?
   B: No, I ______. Why?
   A: Well, you ______ at work, so I wasn't sure.
2. **A:** How ______ the food?
   B: Incredible! There ______ lots of fresh seafood and the fruit ______ delicious.
3. **A:** So ______ your vacation OK?
   B: Well, actually it ______. The food ______ terrible and the people ______ unfriendly. What more can I say?
4. **A:** Where ______ you last weekend?
   B: I ______ on vacation.
   A: Really? How ______ it?
5. **A:** How long ______ your vacation?
   B: Only a week. But you know something? After a week, the kids and I ______ pretty tired.

B **Write questions with the scrambled words.**

1. A: ______________________________?
   your / vacation / was / very long
   B: No, it wasn't. It was pretty short, actually.

2. A: ______________________________?
   your luggage / was / where
   B: My wife had it. I thought someone had stolen it!

3. A: ______________________________?
   the drive / was / comfortable
   B: Perfect.

4. A: ______________________________?
   you / were / on the morning flight
   B: Yes, I was.

UNIT 8 Lesson 2

The simple past tense: usage

Use the simple past tense to talk about a completed action in the past.

My grandparents went to Paris. We played tennis and went running every day.

The simple past tense: form

Regular verbs: spelling rules

Form the past tense of most verbs by adding –ed to the base form.

play → play**ed**

For verbs ending in –e or –ie, add –d.

smile → smile**d** tie → tie**d**

For one-syllable verbs ending in one vowel + one consonant, double the consonant and add –ed.

stop → stop**ped** plan → plan**ned**

Two-syllable verbs ending in one vowel + one consonant: If the first syllable is stressed, add –ed.

vi - sit → visit**ed**

If the second syllable is stressed, double the consonant and add –ed.

pre - fer → prefer**red**

For verbs ending in a consonant and –y, change the –y to –i and add –ed.

study → stud**ied**

Irregular verbs

Do not use –ed. See Appendix page A5 for a list of irregular verbs in the simple past tense form.

Negative statements

Use didn't + the base form of a verb.

He **didn't go** to his grandmother's last weekend.
NOT ~~He didn't goes to his grandmother's last weekend.~~

They **didn't have** a good trip.
NOT ~~They didn't had a good trip.~~

The simple past tense: questions

Begin yes / no questions with Did. Use the base form of the verb.

Did you **go** swimming every day? NOT ~~Did you went swimming every day?~~

Begin information questions with a question word followed by did.

Where did you go shopping? **When did** you leave? **What did** you eat everyday?

A Write the simple past tense form of the following verbs.

1. return *returned*
2. like ________
3. change ________
4. cry ________
5. try ________
6. stay ________
7. travel ________
8. arrive ________
9. rain ________
10. wait ________
11. offer ________
12. hurry ________

B Write the simple past tense form of these irregular verbs.

1. eat *ate*
2. drink ________
3. swim ________
4. go ________
5. write ________
6. meet ________
7. run ________
8. begin ________
9. buy ________
10. read ________
11. pay ________
12. understand ________

C Complete the conversations with questions in the simple past tense. Use a capital letter to begin sentences.

1. **A:** *Where did you go on vacation last summer*?
   you / go / where / on vacation last summer
   B: We went to the mountains. It was very nice.
2. **A:** ________?
   you / get back / when / from vacation
   B: We got back last week. I'm sorry we didn't call you.
3. **A:** ________?
   they / have / a good flight
   B: Well, they said it was really scenic. So I guess so.
4. **A:** ________?
   you / do / what / in London
   B: We went to see some plays and we visited a few museums.
5. **A:** ________?
   your parents / enjoy / their trip
   B: Well, almost. There were some problems, but I think they had a good time.

UNIT 9 Lesson 1

Modals can, should, could: meaning

Use can to express ability or possibility.

Jerome **can** speak Korean. **Can** you be there before 8:00?

Use could to suggest an alternative or to make a weak suggestion.

They **could** see an old movie like *Titanic*, or they **could** go to something new.

Use should to give advice or to express criticism.

You **should** think before you speak.

Modals: form

Modals are followed by the base form of the main verb of the sentence, except in short answers to questions.

Who **should read** this? They **should**. **Can** you **see** the moon tonight? Yes, I **can**.

Never add –s to the third-person singular form of modals.

He **should** buy a ticket in advance. NOT ~~He shoulds buy a ticket in advance.~~

Never use to between modals and the base form.

You **could take** the train or the bus. NOT ~~You could to take the train or the bus.~~

Use not between the modal and the base form.

You **shouldn't stay** at the Galaxy Hotel. They **can't take** the express.

Modals: questions

In yes / no questions, the modal comes before the subject. In information questions, the question word precedes the modal.

yes / no questions	information questions
Should I buy a round-trip ticket?	**Which** trains **could** I take?
Can we make the 1:05 flight?	**Who can** give me the information?
Could she take an express train?	**When should** they leave?

A Complete each sentence or question.

1. Who ______ (should buy / should to buy) the tickets?
2. Where ______ (I can find / can I find) a hotel?
3. You ______ (could to walk / could walk) or ______ (take / taking) the bus.
4. ______ (I should call / Should I call) you when I arrive?
5. We ______ (can to not take / can't take) the bus; it left five minutes ago.
6. When ______ (should you giving / should you give) the agent your boarding pass?
7. Which trains ______ (can get / can getting) me there before dinnertime?

UNIT 9 Lesson 2

Expression of future actions

There are four ways to express future actions using the present tenses. These are similar in meaning.

be going to

be going to + base form usually expresses a future plan or certain knowledge about the future.

I'm **going to spend** my summer in Africa.
She's **going to get** a rental car when she arrives.
It's **going to rain** tomorrow.

The present continuous

The present continuous can also express a future plan.

We'**re traveling** tonight.
They **aren't wearing** formal clothes to the wedding.
We **aren't eating** home tomorrow.

The simple present tense

The simple present tense can express a future action, almost always with verbs of motion: arrive, come, depart, fly, go, head, leave, sail, and start, especially when on a schedule or timetable. When the simple present tense expresses the future, there is almost always a word, phrase, or clause indicating the future time.

This Monday the express **leaves** at noon.

The present tense of be

The present tense of be can describe a future event if it includes a word or phrase that indicates the future.

The wedding **is on Sunday**.

A **Answer the following questions.**

1. What are your plans for the summer?

   ____

2. What are you going to do this weekend?

   ____

3. What are you doing this evening?

   ____

B **Read the arrival and departure schedules. Then complete each question or statement with the simple present tense.**

1. The bus ________ at 11:00. It ________ at 8:00.
2. When ________ the flight ________? At 1:30.
3. The flight ________ at 23:30.
4. What time ________ the train ________ in Beijing? At ten-twenty at night.
5. ________ the train ________ at seven? Yes, it does.

UNIT 10 Lesson 1

Comparison with adjectives

Comparative adjectives compare two people, places, or things.

Mexico City is **bigger than** Los Angeles.

Superlative adjectives compare more than two people, places, or things.

Mexico City is **the biggest** city in the Americas. (compared to all the other cities in the Americas)

adjective	comparative adjective	superlative adjective
cheap	**cheaper (than)**	**the cheapest**
expensive	**more expensive (than)**	**the most expensive**

Superlative adjectives: form

Add –est to one-syllable adjectives. If the adjective ends in –e, add –st. Remember to use the with superlatives.

cheap → **the** cheap**est** loose → **the** loose**st**

If an adjective ends with consonant-vowel-consonant, double the final consonant before adding –est.

hot → the hott**est**

For most adjectives that end in –y, change the y to i and add –est.

pretty → the prett**iest** busy → the bus**iest**

To make the superlative form of most adjectives of two or more syllables, use the most or the least.

Car trips are **the least relaxing** vacations. Safaris are **the most exciting** vacations.

A Write the comparative and superlative form of the following adjectives.

	comparative	superlative
1. tall	________	________
2. easy	________	________
3. liberal	________	________
4. heavy	________	________
5. unusual	________	________
6. pretty	________	________
7. exciting	________	________
8. wild	________	________
9. informal	________	________
10. interesting	________	________
11. conservative	________	________
12. light	________	________
13. casual	________	________
14. comfortable	________	________
15. relaxing	________	________

B Complete each sentence with a comparative or superlative adjective.

1. That dinner was ________ (delicious) meal on our vacation.
2. This scanner is definitely ________ (good) than that one.
3. The Caribbean cruise is ________ (relaxing) of our vacation packages.
4. The Honshu X24 is a good camera, but the Cashio Speedo 5 is ________ (easy) to use.
5. We have several brands, but I'd say the R300 is ________ (popular).
6. Sunday is going to be ________ (bad) day of the week. It's the end of my vacation!
7. I like that vase, but I think this one is ________ (beautiful).
8. The Italian bowl was a good deal, but the Portuguese one was ________ (nice).

C Complete the conversations with a superlative adjective.

1. **A:** Well, we've got several brands to choose from.
   B: Which one's ________ (good)?
2. **A:** Would you like to see these scanners?
   B: Sure. But which one's ________ (easy) to use?
3. **A:** I'm looking for a PDA. Which brand is ________ (light)?
   B: Oh, that would be the Delio P500.
4. **A:** How much can you spend?
   B: Not too much. Which is ________ (expensive)?
5. **A:** I love these plates. They're so unusual. Should we buy one?
   B: Sure. Which one do you think is ________ (attractive)?

UNIT 10 Lesson 2

Intensifiers too, really, and very

Intensifiers make the meaning of adjectives stronger.

Too expresses the idea of "more than enough." Too has a negative meaning.

These shoes are **too** expensive. I'm not going to buy them. That movie is **too** scary. I don't want to see it.

Very and really don't have negative meaning.

These shoes are **very** expensive. I like them. That movie is **really** scary. I'm going to love it.

A Complete each sentence with a phrase using too, really, or very.

1. Beach vacations are _really relaxing_________. I love them.
2. French fries are ______________________. You shouldn't eat them every day.
3. A safari vacation is ______________________. I don't have enough money to go.
4. This movie is ______________________. I want to see it.
5. Our house is ______________________. I don't want to sell it.
6. English is ______________________. Many people study it.
7. This printer is ______________________. I need a new one.
8. Those pants are ______________________! You should wear something more conservative.

B Complete the conversations. Write the adjectives with too or enough.

1. **A:** How about this necklace? Should we buy it for your mother?
   B: No. It isn't ___________ (pretty). I want something nicer.
2. **A:** Look. I bought this rug today. Do you think it's too small?
   B: No. I think it's ___________ (big).
3. **A:** I'm sending this steak back to the chef.
   B: Why? What's wrong?
   A: It's just not ___________ (good).
4. **A:** How was your vacation?
   B: Well, to tell the truth, it just wasn't ___________ (relaxing).
5. **A:** Did you buy a microwave oven?
   B: I looked at some yesterday. But they were ___________ (expensive).
6. **A:** You don't eat candy?
   B: No. It's ___________ (sweet) for me.
7. **A:** How's that soup? Is it ___________ (hot)?
   B: No, it's fine. Thanks.
8. **A:** Do you want any ice in your water?
   B: No, thanks. It's ___________ (cold).

TOP NOTCH POP LYRICS FOR 1A AND 1B

Going Out [Unit 2]

Do you want to see a play?
What time does the play begin?
It starts at eight. Is that OK?
I'd love to go. I'll see you then.
I heard it got some good reviews.
Where's it playing? What's the show?
It's called "One Single Life to Lose."
I'll think about it. I don't know.

(CHORUS)

Everything will be all right
when you and I go out tonight.

When Thomas Soben gives his talk—
The famous chef? That's not for me!
The doors open at nine o'clock.
There's a movie we could see.
at Smith and Second Avenue.
That's my favorite neighborhood!
I can't wait to be with you.
I can't wait to have some food.

(CHORUS)

We're going to have a good time.
Don't keep me up past my bedtime.
We'll make a date.
Tonight's the night.
It starts at eight.
The price is right!
I'm a fan of rock and roll.
Classical is more my style.
I like blues and I like soul.
Bach and Mozart make me smile!
Around the corner and down the street.
That's the entrance to the park.
There's a place where we could meet.
I wouldn't go there after dark!

(CHORUS: 2 times)

The World Café [Unit 5]

Is there something that you want?
Is there anything you need?
Have you made up your mind
what you want to eat?
Place your order now,
or do you need more time?
Why not start with some juice—
lemon, orange, or lime?
Some like it hot, some like it sweet,
some like it really spicy.
You may not like everything you eat,
but I think we're doing nicely.

(CHORUS)

I can understand every word you say.
Tonight we're speaking English at The World Café.

I'll take the main course now.
I think I'll have the fish.
Does it come with a choice of another dish?
Excuse me waiter, please—
I think I'm in the mood
for a little dessert, and the cake looks good.
Do you know? Are there any low-fat
desserts that we could try now?
I feel like having a bowl of fruit.
Do you have to say good-bye now?

(CHORUS)

Apples, oranges, cheese and ham,
coffee, juice, milk, bread, and jam,
rice and beans, meat and potatoes,
eggs and ice cream,
grilled tomatoes—
That's the menu.
That's the list.
Is there anything I missed?

(CHORUS)

A Typical Day [Unit 6]

The Couch Potato sits around.
He eats junk food by the pound.
It's just a typical day.
Watching as the world goes by,
he's out of shape and wonders why.
It's just a typical day.

(CHORUS)

Every night he dreams that he's
skydiving through the air.
And sometimes you appear.
He says, "What are you doing here?"

He cleans the house and plays guitar,
takes a shower, drives the car.
It's just a typical day.
He watches TV all alone,
reads and sleeps, talks on the phone.
It's just a typical day.

(CHORUS)

I'm sorry.
Mr. Couch Potato's resting right now.
Can he call you back?
He usually lies down every day of the week,
and he always has to have a snack.
Now all his dreams are coming true.
He's making plans to be with you.
It's just a typical day.
He goes dancing once a week.
He's at the theater as we speak!
It's just a typical day.

(CHORUS)

My Dream Vacation [Unit 8]

The ride was bumpy
and much too long.
It was pretty boring.
It felt so wrong.
I slept all night,
and it rained all day.
We left the road,
and we lost the way.
Then you came along
and you took my hand.
You whispered words
I could understand.

(CHORUS)

On my dream vacation,
I dream of you.
I don't ever want to wake up.
On my dream vacation,
this much is true:
I don't ever want it to stop.

The food was awful.
They stole my purse.
The whole two weeks went
from bad to worse.
They canceled my ticket.
I missed my flight.
They were so unfriendly
it just wasn't right.
So I called a taxi,
and I got inside,
and there you were,
sitting by my side.

(CHORUS)

You were so unusual.
The day was so exciting.
I opened up my eyes,
and you were gone.
I waited for hours.
You never called.
I watched TV
and looked at the walls.
Where did you go to?
Why weren't you near?
Did you have a reason
to disappear?
So I flew a plane
to the south of France,
and I heard you say,
"Would you like to dance?"

(CHORUS)

Shopping for Souvenirs [Unit 10]

I go to the bank at a quarter to ten.
I pick up my cash from the ATM.
Here at the store, it won't be too hard
to take out a check or a credit card.
The bank has a good rate of exchange,
and everything here is in my price range.
The easiest part of this bargain hunt
is that I can afford anything I want.

(CHORUS)

Whenever I travel around the world,
I spend my money for two.
Shopping for souvenirs
helps me to be near you.

I try to decide how much I should pay
for the beautiful art I see on display.
To get a great deal, I can't be too nice.
It can't hurt to ask for a better price.

(CHORUS)

Yes, it's gorgeous, and I love it.
It's the biggest and the best,
though it might not be the cheapest.
How much is it—more than all the rest?
I'll pass on some good advice to you:
When you're in Rome, do as the Romans do.
A ten percent tip for the taxi fare
should be good enough when you're staying there.

(CHORUS)

Workbook

Joan Saslow ■ Allen Ascher

with Barbara R. Denman

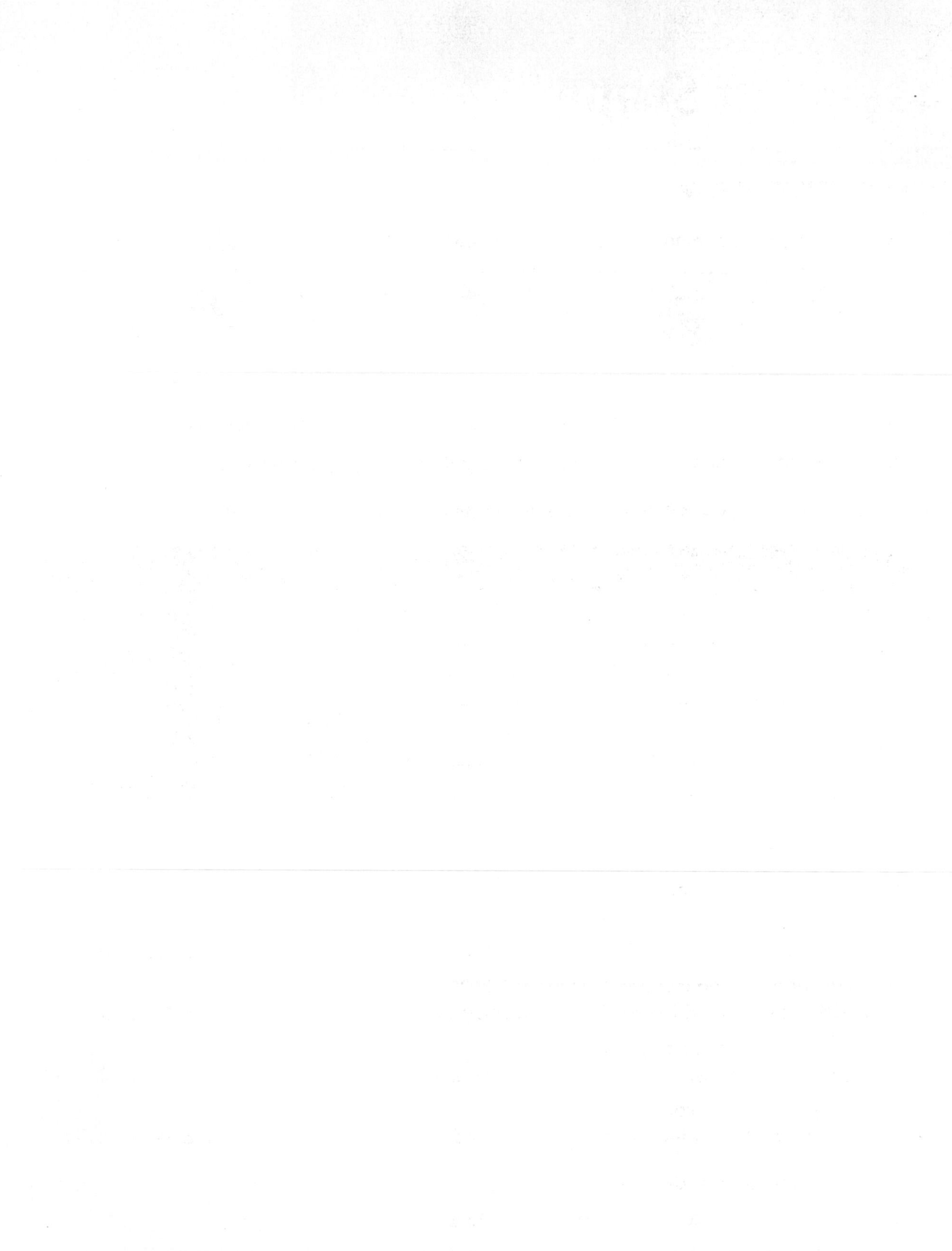

UNIT 6

Staying in Shape

TOPIC PREVIEW

 Look at the pictures. Name each activity. Write the letter on the line.

A  B 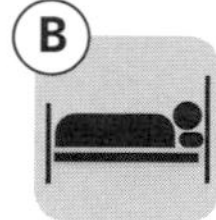 C  D  E  F  G  H  I 

1. ___ swimming
2. ___ walking
3. ___ doing aerobics
4. ___ dancing
5. ___ playing soccer
6. ___ playing the guitar
7. ___ running
8. ___ lifting weights
9. ___ sleeping

 WHAT ABOUT YOU? **How often do you do these activities? Complete the chart.**

Activity	Frequency
ride a bike	
eat in a restaurant	
shop for clothes	
shop for food	
watch TV	
clean your house	
exercise	

LESSON 1

 **Choose the correct response. Circle the letter.**

1. "Can you go walking at 4:30?"
   a. Yes, I am. b. No, I can't. c. Yes, I do.
2. "Why don't we go dancing tonight at 8:00?"
   a. OK. When's good for you? b. Sorry, I can't. c. Too bad.
3. "When do you have to go to work?"
   a. No, I'm not busy. b. How about tomorrow at 6:00? c. At 10:30.
4. "When's good for you?"
   a. How about Monday morning? b. Sounds good! c. Sorry, I can't.

 **Complete the sentences. Use <u>have to</u> or <u>has to</u>.**

1. I ____________ go to class this morning. Do you have my textbook?
2. She can sleep late tomorrow morning. She doesn't ____________ work until 10:30.
3. My brother isn't healthy. He ____________ exercise more.
4. They don't ____________ pick us up at the train station. We can take a taxi.

5. Pete __________ buy a new digital camera. His old one isn't working.
6. Do you __________ work next Saturday?
7. We __________ finish our report before the next sales meeting.

5 Write sentences. Use words from each box.

I My parents My teacher My friend My boss My brother	+	has to don't have to can can't have to doesn't have to	+	work late on Friday. play tennis this weekend. go to school. study English. go shopping this weekend. cook dinner tonight. sleep late tomorrow morning.

1. *My brother doesn't have to study English*.
2. ______________________________.
3. ______________________________.
4. ______________________________.
5. ______________________________.

6 Look at Paula's daily planner. Answer the questions about her schedule.

1. Can Paula go running Saturday morning at 9:00?
   No, she can't. She has to
   study English.
2. What does Paula have to do on Sunday afternoon?
   ____
   ______________________________.
3. Does Paula have to work on Friday?
   ____
   ______________________________.
4. Why can't Paula do aerobics Sunday night at 7:30?
   ____
   ______________________________.
5. Can Paula sleep late on Sunday morning?
   ____
   ______________________________.

Daily Planner

	FRIDAY	SATURDAY	SUNDAY
9:00	Arrive at the office	English class	
11:00			
1:00	Sales meeting	Lunch with Dad	Clean the house
3:00			
5:00	Leave the office	Shop for a new cell phone	Cook dinner
7:00	Do aerobics		See a movie with Sara

7 **Look at the responses. Write questions with can or have to.**

1. **A:** (Gail / speak Polish) *Can Gail speak Polish* ______________________?

   B: No. She speaks English and French.

2. **A:** (you / play basketball tonight) ______________________?

   B: Sure. I'm not busy.

3. **A:** (you / meet your brother at the airport) ______________________?

   B: No, I don't. He's taking a bus.

4. **A:** (I / call you tomorrow) ______________________?

   B: OK. That would be great.

5. **A:** (Frank / buy a new printer) ______________________?

   B: No. He fixed his old one.

6. **A:** (they / take the exam on Friday) ______________________?

   B: Yes, they do. They're studying tonight.

LESSON 2

8 **Complete the sentences with places from the box.**

gym	athletic field	pool	court	track	course

1. The school ______________ is used for a lot of different sports. Students play football and soccer in the fall and baseball in the spring.
2. You can take an aerobics class or use exercise machines at a ______________.
3. The hotel has a tennis ______________ and an 18-hole golf ______________.
4. On Fridays, there are water aerobics classes in the swimming ______________.
5. You can go running or walking on a ______________.

9 **Choose the correct response. Write the letter on the line.**

1. ____ "How often do you do aerobics?"
2. ____ "How often do you go swimming?"
3. ____ "When do you go dancing?"
4. ____ "What are you doing this weekend?"
5. ____ "How come you're not going running tonight?"
6. ____ "Are you studying right now?"

a. Because I'm too busy.
b. I go to the gym once a week.
c. No, I'm not. I'm watching TV.
d. I'm going shopping on Saturday and sleeping late on Sunday.
e. I hardly ever go to the pool.
f. On Friday nights.

 **Look at Dave's activity schedule for September. Then complete the sentences. Circle the letter.**

Dave's Activity Schedule ***September***

Sunday	Monday	Tuesday	Wednesday	Thursday	Friday	Saturday
	1 lift weights at the gym 5:30 PM	2	3 play basketball 7:00 PM	4 lift weights at the gym 5:30 PM	5 study English 8:45 PM	6 lift weights at the gym 5:30 PM
7 clean the house 10:00 AM	8 lift weights at the gym 5:30 PM	9 lift weights at the gym 5:30 PM	10 play basketball 7:00 PM	11 lift weights at the gym 5:30 PM	12 study English 8:45 PM	13 go running at the track 12:00 PM
14 clean the house 10:00 AM	15 go running at the track 7:00 PM	16 lift weights at the gym 5:30 PM	17 play basketball 7:00 PM	18 lift weights at the gym 5:30 PM	19	20 lift weights at the gym 10:00 AM play golf 3:00 PM
21 clean the house 10:00 AM lift weights at the gym 1:00 PM	22 lift weights at the gym 5:30 PM	23 lift weights at the gym 5:30 PM	24 play basketball 7:00 PM	25 lift weights at the gym 5:30 PM	26 study English 8:45 PM	27 go bike riding 5:00 PM
28 clean the house 10:00 AM	29 lift weights at the gym 5:30 PM	30				

1. Dave _______ goes bike riding.
   a. hardly ever **b.** never **c.** always
2. Dave _______ cleans the house on Sundays.
   a. always **b.** sometimes **c.** never
3. Dave lifts weights _______.
   a. once a week **b.** three times a week **c.** once in a while
4. Dave plays basketball ________.
   a. on Tuesdays **b.** on Wednesdays **c.** on weekends
5. Dave usually lifts weights ________.
   a. in the evening **b.** in the morning **c.** in the afternoon
6. Dave goes running _________.
   a. once a month **b.** every weekend **c.** once in a while

11 WHAT ABOUT YOU? **Write sentences about your own activities.**

Examples: *I hardly ever eat in a restaurant* .
I ride a bike once in a while .

1. ______________________________.
2. ______________________________.
3. ______________________________.
4. ______________________________.
5. ______________________________.

12 **Look at the responses. Complete the questions. Use the simple present tense.**

1. How often *does Jim play tennis* ?
   Jim plays tennis every day.
2. How often ______________________________?
   I go walking once in a while.
3. When ______________________________?
   I usually cook dinner at 7:30.
4. When ______________________________?
   They go dancing on Friday nights.
5. Where ______________________________?
   We do aerobics at the gym.
6. Where ______________________________?
   Kyle plays soccer at the athletic field.

13 **Write sentences. Use the simple present tense or the present continuous.**

1. Charlie / usually / play golf / on weekends
   Charlie usually plays golf on weekends .
2. Stan / talk on the phone / right now
   ______________________________.
3. My daughter / never / study English
   ______________________________.
4. We / go dancing / tonight
   ______________________________.
5. I / sleep late / tomorrow morning
   ______________________________.
6. He / take a shower / now
   ______________________________.
7. They / drive to work / at least once a week
   ______________________________.
8. She / work late / next Tuesday
   ______________________________.
9. I / always / go swimming / on Mondays and Wednesdays
   ______________________________.

LESSONS 3 AND 4

Read the letters to a health magazine advice column.

Dear In-Shape,

I have two health questions for you. I'm an athlete. I play baseball for my university team and I go running every day. I exercise all the time. I think I'm in terrific shape, but I'm worried that I exercise too much. That's my first question—how much exercise is too much?

My second question is about my diet. I try to eat healthy. I hardly ever eat pizza, fast food, or other snacks. I never drink soft drinks. But I have one really bad habit: I'm crazy about sweets!

I eat too much chocolate, candy, cake, and ice cream. How can I cut down on sweets?

—Ron Miller

Dear In-Shape,

I need some exercise advice! I don't feel very healthy. I get tired just walking from my house to my car! My doctor said that I have to exercise more. I'm sure that she's right. I should get out of the house more often. My husband goes running every day, but I never go running with him. I'm a couch potato. My big activity is watching movies—I watch a movie just about every night. Unfortunately, you don't burn many calories watching TV!

By the way, the problem is not my diet. I generally try to eat foods that are good for me, like fish, vegetables, and fruit. I avoid snacks and I almost never eat sweets!

—Nina Hunter

Now read the letters again. Complete the chart about Ron and Nina's diet and exercise habits. Check ✔ the boxes.

	Ron Miller	Nina Hunter
is in shape	☐	☐
is out of shape	☐	☐
eats junk food	☐	☐
avoids sweets	☐	☐
has a sweet tooth	☐	☐

15 Read the sentences about Ron and Nina. Check ✔ true, false, or no information.

	true	false	no information
1. Ron doesn't have time to exercise.	☐	☐	☐
2. Ron avoids junk food.	☐	☐	☐
3. Ron usually drinks a lot of water.	☐	☐	☐
4. Nina never eats fish.	☐	☐	☐
5. Nina doesn't exercise regularly.	☐	☐	☐
6. Nina doesn't want to eat healthy foods.	☐	☐	☐

16 WHAT ABOUT YOU? Are you in shape? Do you have a healthy diet? Explain your answers.

Example: *I don't have a healthy diet. I almost never eat vegetables . . .*

GRAMMAR BOOSTER

A **Look at the responses. Write information questions with can.**

1. A: *Where can I go running* ________________________?
   B: Well, you can run in the park.
2. A: ________________________?
   B: I think she can come after class, but I'm not sure.
3. A: ________________________?
   B: Three. I speak Spanish, English, and Japanese.
4. A: ________________________?
   B: I can meet you at 9:30.
5. A: ________________________?
   B: Not very often. Golf is so expensive around here.

B **Look at the responses. Write information questions with have to.**

1. A: *How often do you have to* ________________ see your doctor?
   B: Not very often. Just once a year.
2. A: ________________ meet the client tomorrow?
   B: I have to meet him at the airport.
3. A: ________________ pick up the car?
   B: You have to pick it up before 5:00. They close early today.
4. A: ________________ work late tonight?
   B: Because she has a big meeting tomorrow.
5. A: ________________ get at the supermarket?
   B: We need to get some chicken and onions for dinner tonight.

C **Complete the sentences. Circle the letter.**

1. I ____________ about lunch. What do you want?
   a. think **b.** am thinking **c.** thinks
2. He ____________ her very much now.
   a. love **b.** is loving **c.** loves
3. Michelle can't come to the phone. She ____________.
   a. sleep **b.** sleeping **c.** is sleeping
4. They ____________ the chef at that restaurant.
   a. are knowing **b.** know **c.** am knowing
5. We ____________ some soup for dinner. Do you want some?
   a. am having **b.** has **c.** are having

 **Write sentences in the simple present tense.**

1. she / a lot / swimming / not / go

   She doesn't go swimming a lot ______.

2. walk / Joel / to school / every day

   ______.

3. every week / not / my sisters / me / call

   ______.

4. every day / meet / not / their class

   ______.

5. they / play tennis / three times a week

   ______.

JUST FOR **FUN**

 **Complete the crossword puzzle.**

Across

1. don't do something because it's bad for you
2. where you play tennis
3. ball game popular around the world
4. a place for indoor exercise
5. 0% of the time

Down

1. 100% of the time
6. where "potatoes" sit
7. exercise on a bike
8. the foods you eat
9. where you play golf

 **Which game or sport uses these? Write the activity or sport on the line.**

1. ______________________ 2. ______________________ 3. ______________________

4. ______________________ 5. ______________________ 6. ______________________

What is the number one sport in the world? Many people say soccer is the world's most popular sport. In 2002, 1.5 billion watched the World Cup soccer games on TV. That's one out of every four people in the world!

A JOKE FOR YOU!

UNIT 7

Finding Something to Wear

TOPIC PREVIEW

1 Look at the shopping website. Which department would you click to buy these clothing items? Match the department with the item. Write the letter on the line.

1. F
2. ____
3. ____
4. ____
5. ____
6. ____
7. ____

Shop at Home Online Department Store

Large selection of fine brand-name clothes FOR THE WHOLE FAMILY!

shop at home ONLINE DEPARTMENT STORE

". . Just click your mouse. Stay in your house."®

SIGN IN | REGISTER | MY ACCOUNT | CUSTOMER SERVICE | CHECKOUT | VIEW CART

SPECIALS | OUTERWEAR | HOSIERY | SLEEPWEAR | BAGS and ACCESSORIES | ATHLETIC WEAR

DEPARTMENTS

- Bags and Accessories
- Men's Underwear
- Men's Sleepwear
- Hosiery
- Women's Sleepwear
- Athletic Wear
- Outerwear

SEARCH GO

THIS WEEK'S SPECIALS
Click on items for special prices and other details.

A Jackets
B Socks and Tights
C Men's Boxers
D Men's Pajamas
E Nightgowns
F Leather Bags and Belts
G Running Shoes, Shorts, and Sweatpants

HOME | OTHER PRODUCTS & SERVICES | GIFT CARDS | CATALOGS | ABOUT US | CONTACT US

2 What's important to these customers when they shop for footwear? Write price, selection, or service on the line.

I always shop at Dalton's Department Store because the clerks are really helpful. They always help me find the right size and even offer to gift wrap!

1. ________________

I'm a student so I don't have a lot of money. I shop at Shoe Outlet because they always have a big sale. The shoes I'm wearing now were 50% off!

2. ________________

Jake's Footwear is the best! They have more than 200 different kinds of footwear—boots, sandals, running shoes . . . I like to have a lot of choices when I shop.

3. ________________

LESSON 1

Choose the correct response. Circle the letter.

1. "Do you have this in a medium?"
   a. No, thanks. b. Yes, here you go. c. Yes, please.
2. "See if these are larger."
   a. Yes, they're OK. b. They're $39. c. That's too bad.
3. "How much are the pajamas?"
   a. The Sleepy brand ones? b. They're too small. c. This one's a medium.
4. "Can I try it on?"
   a. Of course! b. No, I'm sorry. We don't. c. We have a smaller size in black.

Complete the chart with words from the box. Write the comparative form of each adjective in the correct column.

loose	spicy	hot	sweet	comfortable
tall	bad	important	thin	young
friendly	healthy	nice	fat	convenient

1. (+) -r	2. (+) -er	3. (-) -y (+) -ier	4. double the final consonant (+) -er	5. more	6. irregular forms
larger	*smaller*	*heavier*	*bigger*	*more expensive*	*better*
					X
X					X

Compare the items in the pictures. Write sentences with comparative adjectives. Use words from the box or your own words.

spicy	salty	expensive	portable	young
old	cheap	fast	healthy	large
big	small	comfortable	good	convenient

1. 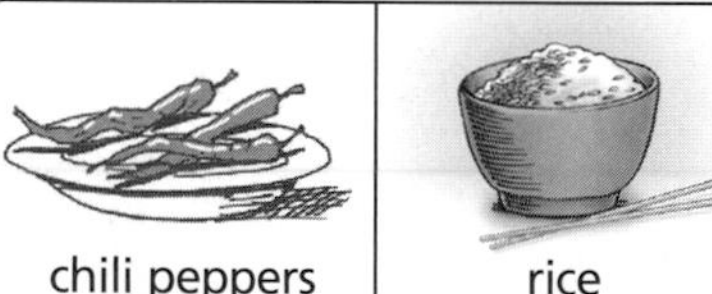
chili peppers | rice
Chili peppers are spicier than rice.

2. 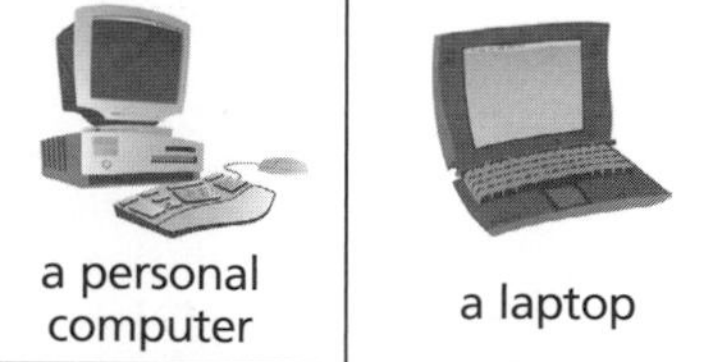
a personal computer | a laptop
______________________________.

3. 
a hair dryer | a photocopier
______________________________.

4. running shoes / pumps ______________________________.

5. your grandparents / your children ______________________________.

6. a salad / french fries ______________________________.

7. a microwave oven / a conventional oven ______________________________.

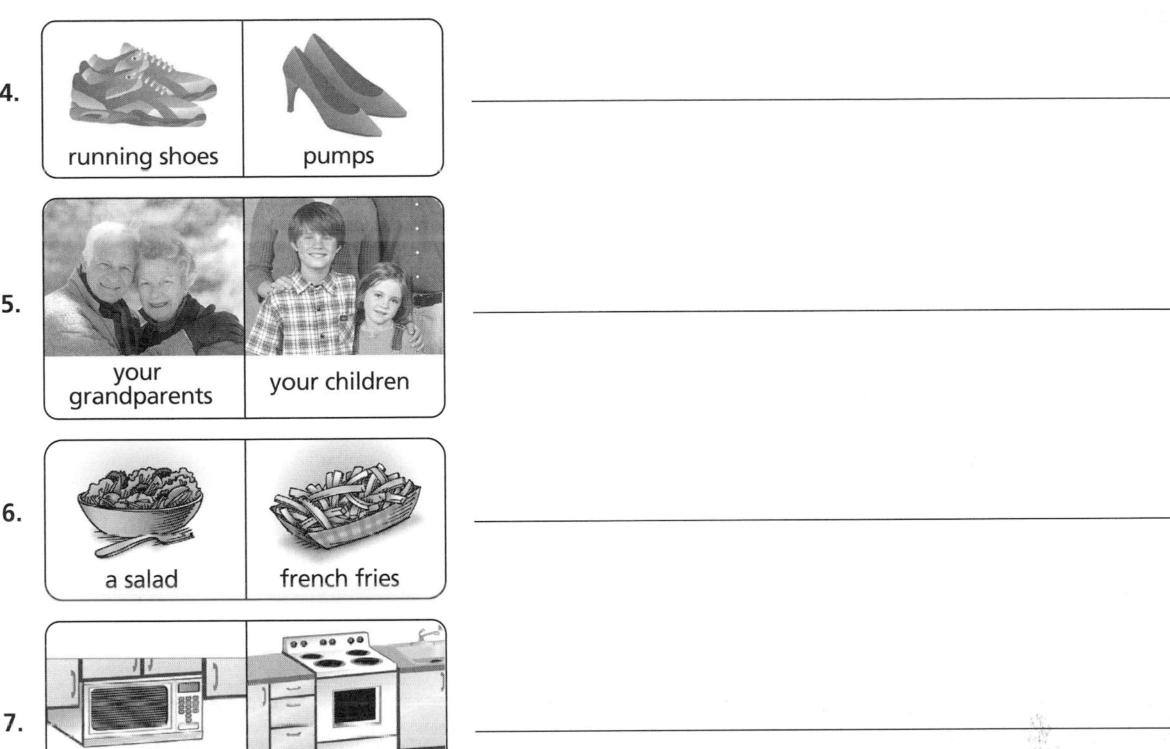

6 **Look at the store ad. Then complete the sentences. Use the information in the ad or your <u>own</u> words.**

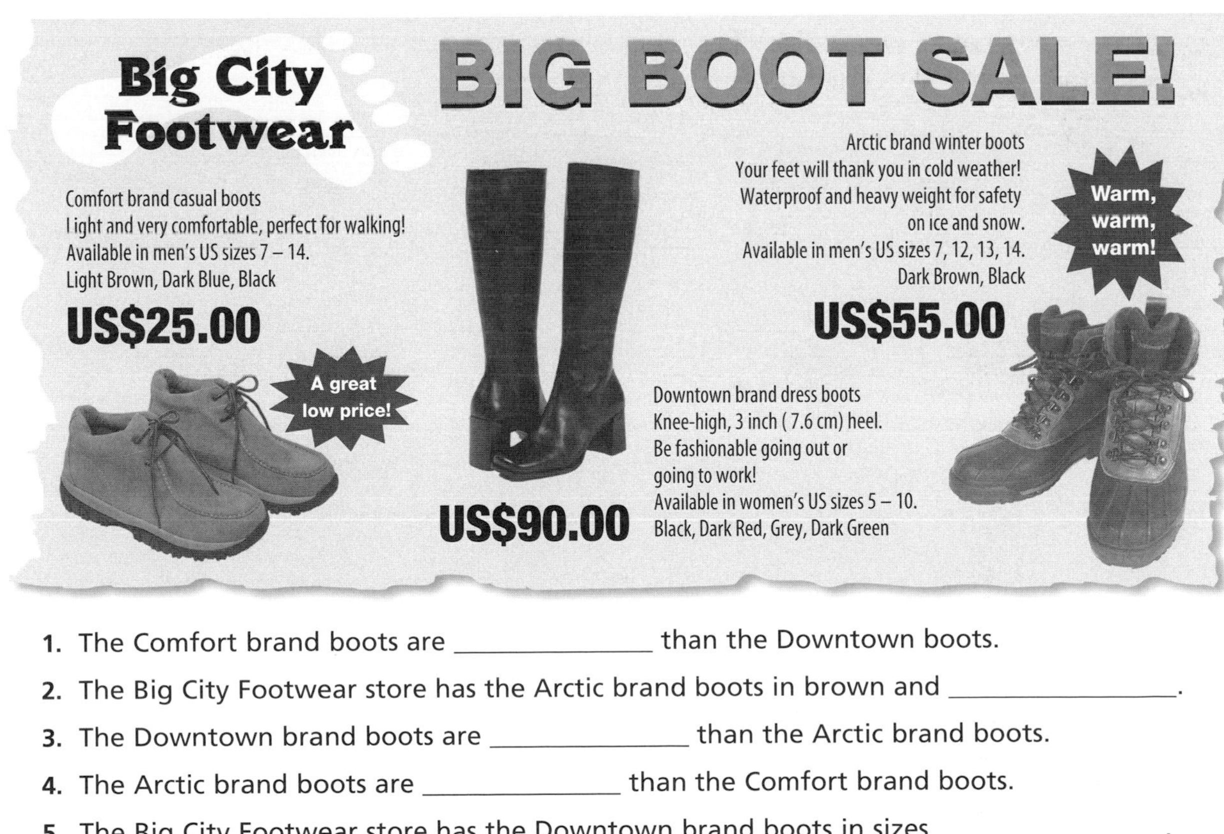

1. The Comfort brand boots are ______________ than the Downtown boots.
2. The Big City Footwear store has the Arctic brand boots in brown and ______________.
3. The Downtown brand boots are ______________ than the Arctic brand boots.
4. The Arctic brand boots are ______________ than the Comfort brand boots.
5. The Big City Footwear store has the Downtown brand boots in sizes ______________.

7 WHAT ABOUT YOU? **Complete the sentences. Use your <u>own</u> ideas and the cues in parentheses.**

1. A ______________ is more expensive than a ______________. (two electronic products)
2. ______________ is too spicy for me. (food)
3. The movie ______________ is better than ______________. (two movies)
4. ______________ is more beautiful than ______________. (two actresses)
5. ______________ is warmer than ______________ in my city. (two months)
6. A size ______________ shoe is too large for me. (a shoe size)

LESSON 2

8 **Complete the conversations. Use sentences from the box.**

Certainly.	Charge, please.	The V-neck or the crew neck?	That's too bad.

How would you like to pay?

2. ______________

Did you know that . . .

- the first known pictures of footwear are boots in a 15,000-year-old painting in a cave in Spain?
- in the year 200, Marcus Aurelius, Emperor of Rome, said that only he could wear red sandals?
- before the 1860s, pairs of boots didn't have a right and a left? Both boots were the same.

9 **Label the clothing items in the picture. Use words from the box.**

pumps
running shoes
a sweatshirt
a blazer
a shirt
a windbreaker
pantyhose
a skirt
socks
sweatpants

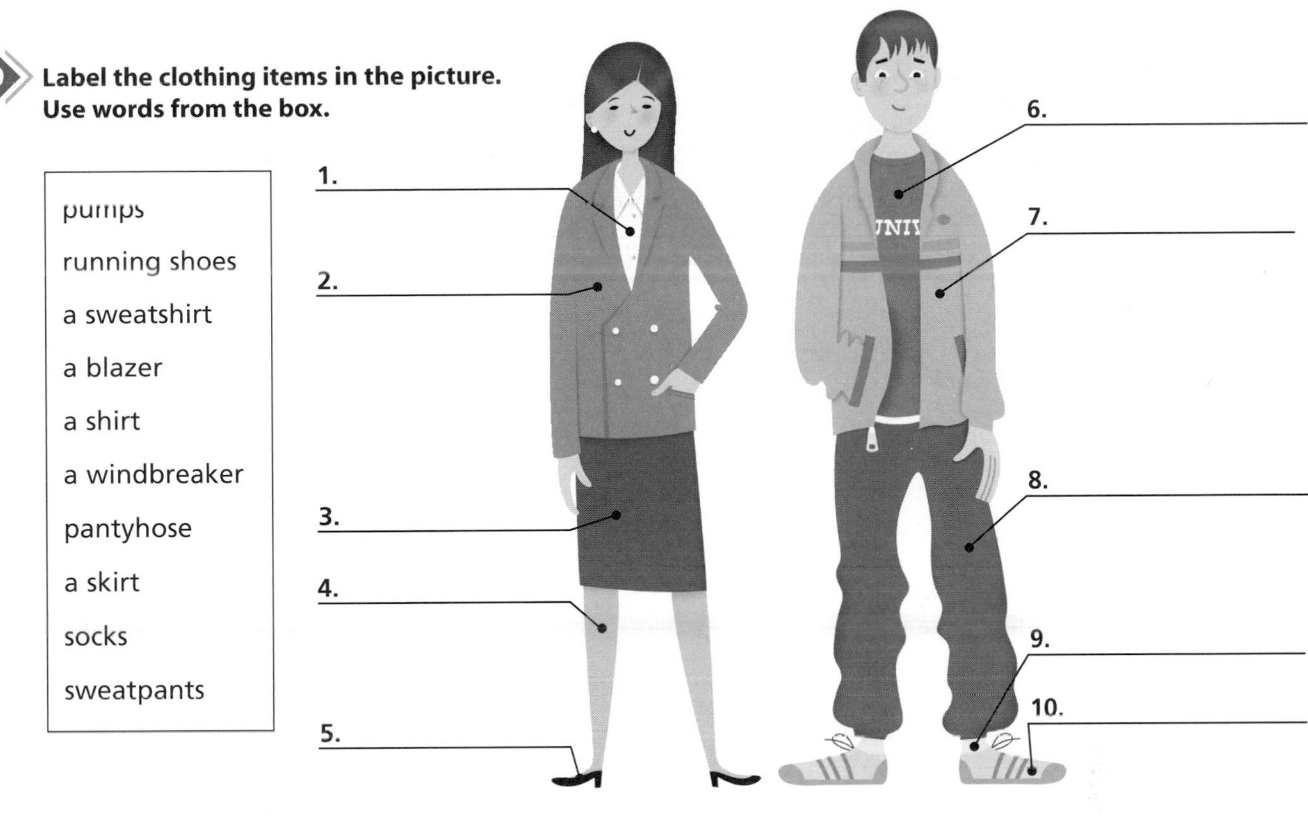

10 WHAT ABOUT YOU? **What's your style? Complete the chart with the clothing and shoes you usually wear.**

At home	At work	At school

11 **Complete the conversations. Use object pronouns from the box. Pronouns can be used more than once.**

me you him her it us you them

1. **A:** Are your sisters going to the party?
   B: I hope so. I invited __________.
2. **A:** This sweatshirt is really old.
   B: That's OK. I wear __________ to exercise.
3. **A:** Did you meet Ms. Jacobs?
   B: Yes, I met __________ this morning.
4. **A:** When can I call you?
   B: Let's see. Call __________ tomorrow. I'll be home all day.
5. **A:** I didn't see you and Emma at the concert.
   B: You didn't see __________? We were right near the stage!
6. **A:** I'll take the sandals.
   B: Great! Would you like me to gift wrap __________ for __________?
7. **A:** These pants are too small.
   B: Give __________ to your brother.
   A: I can't give __________ to __________. He wears a size 32!

LESSONS 3 AND 4

12 **Look at the store floor plan. Start at the Information desk. Follow the directions. Where are you? Write the name of the department on the line.**

1. Go to Women's Casual. Turn right and go straight. It's on the left side, after Hosiery.

   Where are you?

   ____

2. Go to the back of the store. Take the elevator to the basement. It's across from the elevator, straight ahead.

   Where are you?

   ____

3. Take the elevator to the second floor. Turn left and go to Men's Outerwear. Turn right. Go straight. It's between the Men's Shoes and the Men's Sleepwear departments.

   Where are you?

   ____

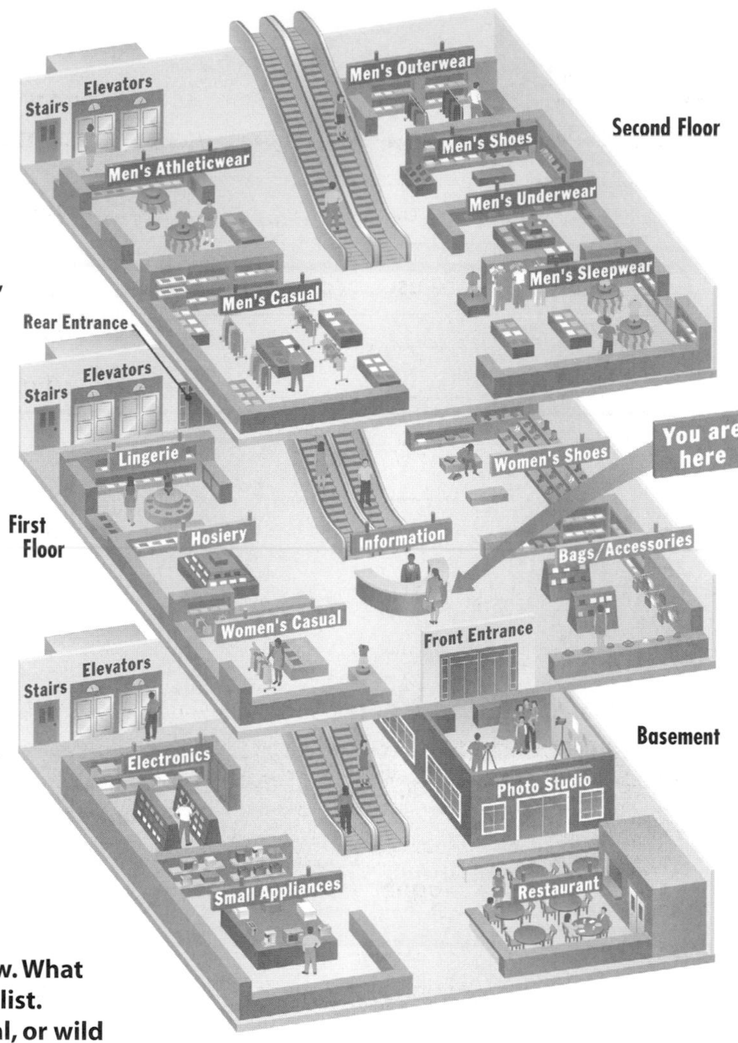

13 **Choose one of the travel destinations below. What clothing will you pack for the trip? Make a list. Include any shoes, outerwear, casual, formal, or wild clothes you will need.**

Go skiing in the Swiss Alps.

Hear gospel music at a Harlem church in New York City, USA.

Go dancing at a nightclub in Paris, France.

Go swimming on Boracay Island, Philippines.

GRAMMAR BOOSTER

A **Complete the sentences with words from the box. Use the comparative form.**

comfortable	expensive	fast	large	healthful	warm	old	~~short~~

1. Women are usually *shorter than* ________ men.
2. A coat is ____________ a sweater.
3. Cars are ____________ radios.
4. Your grandmother is ____________ your nephew.
5. Russia is ____________ Spain.
6. Airplanes are ____________ boats.
7. Sweatpants are ____________ suits.
8. Fruit is ____________ junk food.

B WHAT ABOUT YOU? **Answer the questions in complete sentences. Use your own words.**

1. "Who is taller, you or your best friend?"
   YOU ____.
2. "Who is bigger, your father or your mother?"
   YOU ____.
3. "Which building is bigger, your home or your school?"
   YOU ____.
4. "Which language is easier to learn, your native language or English?"
   YOU ____.
5. "Which is more fun, playing golf or going dancing?"
   YOU ____.

C **Write questions. Use object pronouns and the words in parentheses.**

1. **A:** I take my mother to the same restaurant every week.
   B: *Where do you take her* ____________________? (where)
2. **A:** She washes her car a lot.
   B: ____? (when)
3. **A:** He eats fish.
   B: ____? (how often)
4. **A:** My teacher invites her students to her house.
   B: ____? (why)
5. **A:** Monica meets her boyfriend every morning.
   B: ____? (what time)

 **Write sentences in two ways using the words indicated. Add prepositions if necessary.**

1. the address / give / her

   Give her the address. *Give the address to her*.

2. Tina / gifts / him / buys

   ____________________. ____________________.

3. the teacher / homework / us / gives

   ____________________. ____________________.

4. the waiters / them / food / serve

   ____________________. ____________________.

JUST FOR **FUN**

Look at the pictures. Find the names of the items of clothing in the puzzle. Circle the ten words. Words can be across (→) or down (↓).

s	w	e	a	(b	o	x	e	r	s)	o	s
l	p	n	t	a	s	o	k	n	o	s	w
b	e	i	s	g	n	a	g	r	c	a	e
o	m	g	h	x	t	i	s	t	k	o	a
x	i	h	p	a	j	a	m	a	s	b	t
y	n	t	w	i	n	r	b	r	z	e	p
t	i	g	h	t	s	u	o	u	p	a	a
s	h	o	r	t	s	n	x	n	a	n	n
b	a	w	z	o	p	a	l	b	e	l	t
w	i	n	d	b	r	e	a	k	e	r	s

A Riddle for You!

Riddle: Mr. and Mrs. Bigger had a baby. Which one is the biggest?

Answer: The baby. He's a little Bigger.

UNIT 8

Getting Away

TOPIC PREVIEW

1 **Match the vacation words on the left with their meanings on the right. Write the letter on the line.**

1. ____ wildlife	a. travel by ship or boat
2. ____ accommodations	b. drinks
3. ____ beverages	c. movies, concerts, plays
4. ____ entertainment	d. food
5. ____ meals	e. hotels, hostels, resorts
6. ____ cruise	f. animals
7. ____ rates	g. the money you pay

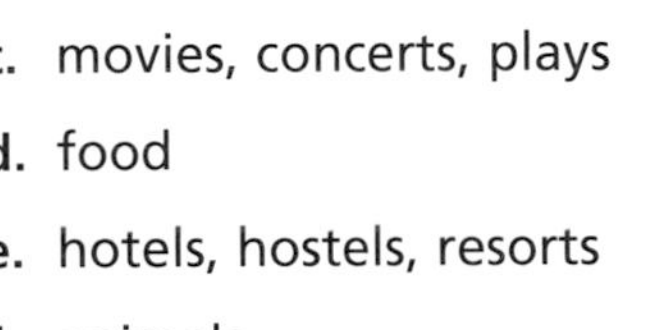

2 WHAT ABOUT YOU? **In your country, where would you go on vacation for . . .**

nature and wildlife?	history and culture?
family activities?	physical activities?

3 WHAT ABOUT YOU? **Complete the paragraph. Use your own ideas.**

When I go on vacation, I usually go to ________________.
I like to visit ________________ and see ________________.
I like to eat ________________. I don't really like to ________________.

LESSON 1

 **Complete the conversations. Write the best response on the lines. Use sentences from the box.**

No, thanks.	That's too bad.	Pretty boring.	Well, that's good.	No, not too bad.

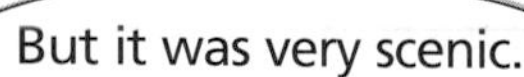

5 **Write statements. Use the words in parentheses and was, were, wasn't, or weren't.**

1. (The cruise / terrific) The cruise was terrific ______.
2. (The accommodations / pretty nice) ______.
3. (Our room / a little small) ______.
4. (There / not / any good family activities) ______.
5. (There / a lot of friendly people) ______.
6. (The flight / not / very long) ______.

6 **Write yes / no questions and short answers. Use the past tense of be.**

1. A: (your / bus / on time) Was your bus on time ______?
   B: No, it wasn't ______. It was over an hour late!
2. A: (the movie theater / open) ______?
   B: Yes, ______. They had a late show.
3. A: (the weather / good) ______?
   B: No, ______. It rained every day.
4. A: (there / a movie / on your flight) ______?
   B: No, ______. It was so boring!
5. A: (there / any problems / at the airport) ______?
   B: Yes, ______. My flight was canceled.

7 **Complete the conversation with information questions. Use the past tense of be.**

A: Hey, Marty. ______?
1. Where / you / last weekend

B: My wife and I took a little vacation.

A: Really? ______?
2. How / it

B: Too short! But we stayed at a great resort.

A: Oh yeah? ______?
3. Where / the resort

B: Over in Wroxton. We drove down Friday night.

A: Wroxton? That's pretty far.
______?
4. How long / the drive

B: About three-and-a-half hours. There wasn't any traffic.

A: Nice! ______?
5. And / how / the weather

B: Actually, the weather was pretty good. Only rained once!

A: Sounds wonderful.
______?
6. How long / you / there

B: Just three days. We didn't want to come home!

8 WHAT ABOUT YOU? **Read the questions. Write responses. Use your own words.**

1. "When was your last vacation?"

   YOU ______________________________

   ______________________________.

2. "How long was it?"

   YOU ______________________________

   ______________________________.

3. "How was the weather?"

   YOU ______________________________

   ______________________________.

MOST POPULAR VACATION

According to the World Tourism Organization, the world's most popular vacation destination is France. In 2001, 76.5 million international visitors came to France. That was 11% of all international travelers! It was also more than the population of France, which was around 60 million. Spain was second, with 49.5 million visitors, and the U.S. was in third place, with 45.5 million.

SOURCE: www.guinnessworldrecords.com

LESSON 2

Complete the chart with the present or the simple past tense.

	Present tense	Simple past tense
1.	call	
2.		arrived
3.		studied
4.	get	
5.	stop	

	Present tense	Simple past tense
6.		went
7.	buy	
8.	do	
9.	leave	
10.		ate

10 **Choose the correct responses to complete the conversation. Write the letter on the line.**

A: Hi, Emily. I didn't see you at the gym this weekend.

B: ___ 1.

A: Really? How was it?

B: ___ 2.

A: What did you do?

B: ___ 3.

A: That sounds nice. Did the kids have a good time?

B: ___ 4.

a. We went to the zoo and ate lunch downtown.

b. Yes, they did. They love nature and wildlife. And they slept all the way home in the car!

c. I didn't go. We took the kids to Toronto.

d. Terrific. We had a lot of fun.

11 **Complete the sentences with the simple past tense.**

1. I ________ (buy) some nice souvenirs, but I ________ (not spend) a lot of money.
2. We ________ (fly) to Montreal, but we ________ (take) the train back.
3. We ________ (have) a great time at the baseball game! The kids ________ (eat) sandwiches and ________ (drink) soda, and they ________ (watch) the game, too—a little!
4. I ________ (leave) at 10:00. I ________ (get) back at noon.

12 **Read the responses. Put the words in order to make questions.**

1. A: (did / eat / Where / you) *Where did you eat* ________?
   B: At a Japanese restaurant.
2. A: (Did / go / with Jane / you) ________?
   B: No, I went with Deanna.
3. A: (like / Did / the art exhibit / you) ________?
   B: No, I didn't. It was pretty boring.
4. A: (you / did / When / leave) ________?
   B: We left on Tuesday morning.
5. A: (What / she / buy / did) ________?
   B: She bought a souvenir T-shirt.
6. A: (did / play tennis / Where / you) ________?
   B: At the resort.
7. A: (did / How long / stay / you) ________?
   B: A little over a month.

13 WHAT ABOUT YOU? **Read the questions. Write a response. Use your own words.**

1. "Did you sleep late this morning?"

   YOU ________.
2. "Where did you eat lunch yesterday?"

   YOU ________.
3. "When did you exercise this week?"

   YOU ________.

LESSONS 3 AND 4

14 **Look at the vacation picture.**

Now read the statements. Who is speaking? Match each statement to a person in the picture. Write the letter on the line.

1. We wanted to go on a cruise, but they canceled it. There was a problem with the boat. _____

2. Someone stole my bag! I lost all of my money and my passport. _____

3. I went parasailing. A boat pulled me up high in the air. It was so exciting! _____

4. I got a massage on the beach. It was so relaxing! _____

5. The entertainment was terrible. They only had one musician—and he needed guitar lessons! _____

6. The local beverages were delicious. I had a drink made of coconut milk every day at the beach. _____

15 Complete the vacation postcard. Use adjectives from the box.

scary	relaxing	perfect	terrible	scenic	unusual

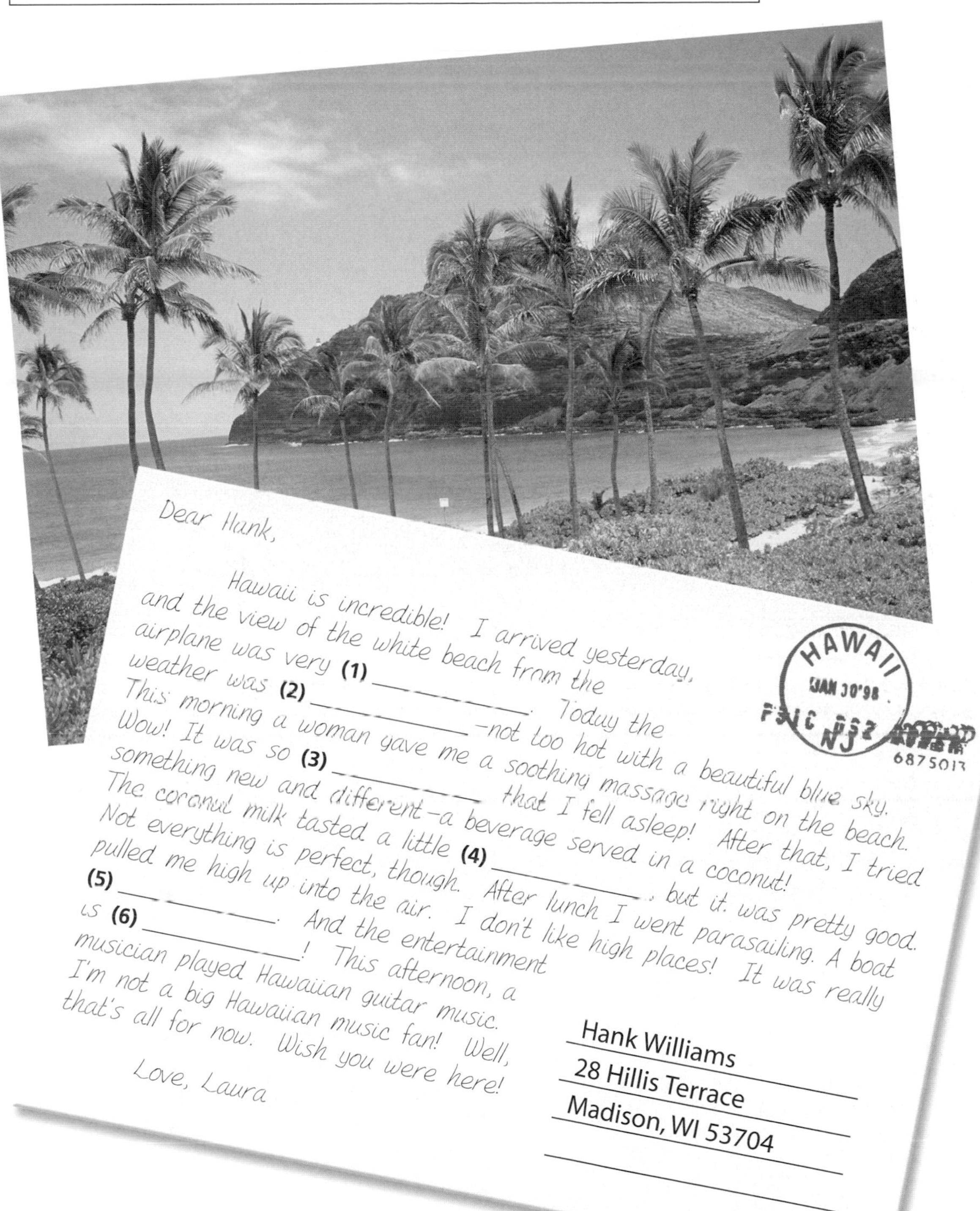

Dear Hank,

Hawaii is incredible! I arrived yesterday, and the view of the white beach from the airplane was very **(1)** __________. Today the weather was **(2)** __________—not too hot with a beautiful blue sky. This morning a woman gave me a soothing massage right on the beach. Wow! It was so **(3)** __________ that I fell asleep! After that, I tried something new and different—a beverage served in a coconut! The coconut milk tasted a little **(4)** __________, but it was pretty good. Not everything is perfect, though. After lunch I went parasailing. A boat pulled me high up into the air. I don't like high places! It was really **(5)** __________. And the entertainment is **(6)** __________! This afternoon, a musician played Hawaiian guitar music. I'm not a big Hawaiian music fan! Well, that's all for now. Wish you were here!

Love, Laura

Hank Williams
28 Hillis Terrace
Madison, WI 53704

GRAMMAR BOOSTER

Choose the correct response. Write the letter on the line.

1. ____ "How was your vacation?"
2. ____ "Where did you go?"
3. ____ "How long were you there?"
4. ____ "Was the weather good?"
5. ____ "How were the accommodations?"
6. ____ "Were there a lot of things to do?"
7. ____ "Was the food OK?"

a. No, it wasn't. It rained all week.
b. Terrific. It was so much fun.
c. Jamaica.
d. Yes, there were. We were busy all the time.
e. Yes, it was good. But a little spicy.
f. Just a week.
g. Clean and comfortable.

Correct the errors in the e-mail message.

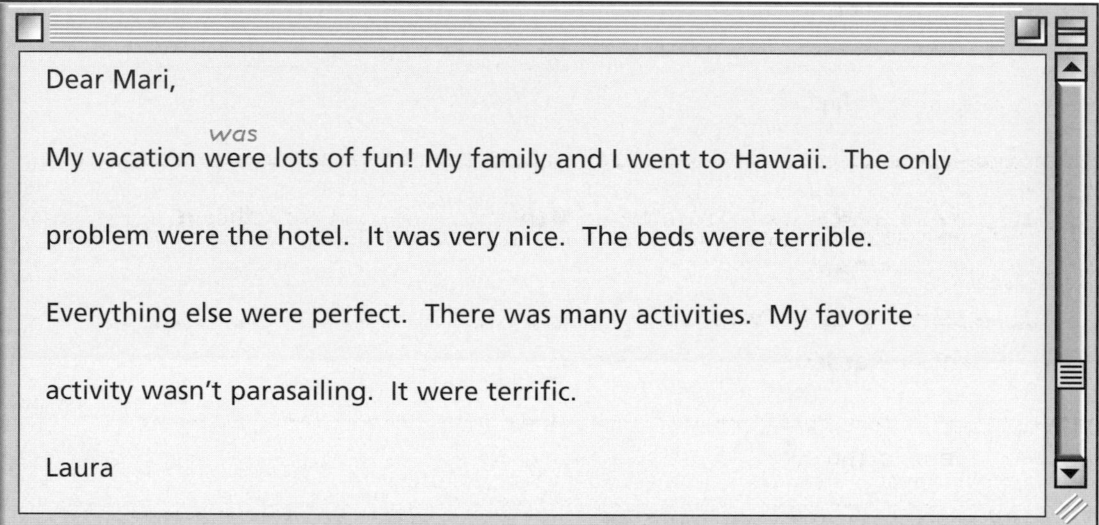

Dear Mari,

was
My vacation were lots of fun! My family and I went to Hawaii. The only problem were the hotel. It was very nice. The beds were terrible. Everything else were perfect. There was many activities. My favorite activity wasn't parasailing. It were terrific.

Laura

WHAT ABOUT YOU? **Write questions with the past tense of <u>be</u>. Then answer the questions with complete sentences. Use your <u>own</u> words.**

1. when / your last vacation ______________________________?
   YOU ______________________________.
2. it / long ______________________________?
   YOU ______________________________.
3. how / the hotel ______________________________?
   YOU ______________________________.
4. the weather / good ______________________________?
   YOU ______________________________.
5. how many / people / with you ______________________________?
   YOU ______________________________.

D **Rewrite the sentences. Use the simple past tense and a past time expression.**

1. We go to the beach every year.
   We went to the beach last year __________.
2. The weather isn't very good today.
   ____________________.
3. How long does the trip usually take?
   ____________________?
4. We don't stay in a hotel.
   ____________________.
5. I often cook clams at the beach.
   ____________________.
6. Everyone has a good time.
   ____________________.
7. Is your flight canceled?
   ____________________?

E **Read the statements. Write questions in response using the words in parentheses.**

1. **A:** She bought a new printer.
   B: *Why did she buy a new printer* __________? (why)
2. **A:** We went on vacation.
   B: ____________________? (where)
3. **A:** They went to the gym.
   B: ____________________? (when)
4. **A:** I visited some friends.
   B: ____________________? (who)
5. **A:** He spent a lot of money.
   B: ____________________? (how much)

JUST FOR **FUN**

 **Find the words in the puzzle. Circle the words. Words can be across (→) or down (↓).**

- scenic
- amazing
- relaxing
- interesting
- boring
- bumpy
- unusual
- short
- comfortable
- long
- exciting
- incredible

l	v	s	c	e	n	i	c	b	c	s	q	a
k	m	w	q	o	x	l	q	g	o	v	b	l
l	h	n	b	e	k	o	w	x	m	c	g	s
r	e	l	a	x	i	n	g	q	f	d	q	x
l	p	o	e	c	p	g	r	e	o	f	g	k
q	g	d	f	i	x	l	f	m	r	t	i	l
s	s	i	n	t	e	r	e	s	t	i	n	g
t	h	x	d	i	n	t	t	b	a	g	c	m
b	o	r	i	n	g	v	y	u	b	s	r	y
u	r	c	c	g	b	c	k	l	l	m	e	c
m	t	b	q	l	j	y	o	p	e	v	d	l
p	p	a	m	a	z	i	n	g	h	r	i	g
y	m	j	l	p	a	m	a	s	y	v	b	o
v	a	y	d	b	u	n	u	s	u	a	l	l
b	x	f	k	t	x	l	h	u	a	f	e	y

 **What can you do in your free time? Unscramble the underlined words. Write the activity on the line.**

1. visit the ozo = *visit the zoo*
2. see a labbasel meag = ______________
3. visit an tar semumu = ______________
4. do bacseori = ______________
5. play fgol = ______________
6. take a ruisce = ______________
7. go on a rasfai = ______________

UNIT 9

Taking Transportation

TOPIC PREVIEW

1 **Look at the departure schedule and the clock. Read the statements. Check ✓ true or false.**

	true	false
1. The next flight to Porto Alegre is at 5:50 p.m.	☐	☐
2. Flight 902 to São Luis is leaving from Gate G4.	☐	☐
3. The flight to Caracas is delayed.	☐	☐
4. Flight number 267 is going to Belo Horizonte.	☐	☐
5. Passengers on Flight 56 are taking Asiana Airline.	☐	☐
6. Flight 60 is late.	☐	☐

RAPID AIR BRASILIA DEPARTURES

Destination	FLT/No.	Departs	Gate	Status
São Paulo	56	15:50	G4	departed
Belo Horizonte	267	16:10	G3	boarding
Rio de Janeiro	89	16:10	G9	boarding
São Paulo	58	16:50	G4	now 17:25
São Luis	902	17:00	G3	on time
São Paulo	60	17:50	G4	delayed
Porto Alegre	763	17:50	G3	on time
Caracas	04	18:05	G1	canceled
Rio de Janeiro	91	18:10	G9	on time
São Paulo	62	18:50	G4	on time

15:50

2 **Choose the correct response. Write the letter on the line.**

1. ____ "Oh, no! The train's leaving in four minutes."
2. ____ "I took Northern Airlines to Hong Kong."
3. ____ "I'm looking for the departure gate."
4. ____ "Are you taking the 8:30 train?"
5. ____ "How often do you fly?"

a. Really? How was the flight?
b. Once or twice a year.
c. Yes, I am. You too?
d. Which one?
e. We should hurry!

3 **Put the conversation in order. Write the number on the line.**

_1_ Can I help you?
___ Let's see. The local leaves from track 23, lower level.
___ That sounds OK. What's the track number?
___ Oh, no! What should I do?
___ Yes. Can I still make the 10:05 express train to Antwerp?
___ Sorry, you missed it.
___ Well, you could take a local train. There's one at 11:05.
___ Thanks very much.

LESSON 1

Choose the correct response. Circle the letter.

1. "I missed the 7:30. What should I do?"
   a. No, I'm sorry. b. You could take the 9:10. c. It left five minutes ago.
2. "The next bus is at 5:50."
   a. Is it an express? b. Is it a direct flight? c. One way or round trip?
3. "One way or round trip?"
   a. Two tickets, please. b. Yes, please. c. One way.
4. "Oh, no! The train is leaving in three minutes!"
   a. No, I'm sorry. b. No, you couldn't. c. We should hurry!

Read the article. Choose the correct answer.

Traveling by Bullet

The Japanese Shinkansen, or "bullet trains," began service in 1964. They carried passengers between Tokyo and Osaka. The first trains traveled at 210 km per hour. Today, shinkansen trains on Japan's main island of Honshu connect Tokyo with most of the larger cities. They travel at speeds between 240 and 300 km per hour. In 2007, the Japanese Railway is going to introduce a 350 km-per-hour train. One tip for bullet train travelers: Get to your departure gate on time. Shinkansen trains are almost never late. In 1999, the average lateness per train was twenty-four seconds!

SOURCE: www.jrtr.net

1. A shinkansen is
   a. a city in Japan.
   b. a train station.
   c. a fast Japanese train.
2. Japanese bullet trains are
   a. always late.
   b. almost always on time.
   c. often canceled.

6 **Complete each sentence or question. Use could or should and the base form of the verb.**

1. Want my advice? ________ (You / take) the express. ________ (You / take) the local, but it takes thirty minutes longer.
2. ________ (You / hurry)! ________ (You / make) the 7:30!
3. ________ (She / buy) round-trip tickets. They are cheaper than two one-way tickets, and she won't have to wait in another ticket line.
4. ________ (We / take) an aisle seat in the rear of the plane or a window seat in the front. What do you think? What seats ________ (we / take)?
5. The flight is delayed. ________ (We / be) late for the meeting. ________ (we / call) the office?
6. No, ________ (they / not / get) a direct flight. They tried, but all the flights had a stop in Anchorage.

 **Look at the schedules. Which train should the people take? Write your advice on the line.**

Metropolitan Railroad			
	Local	**Express**	**Local**
White Plains	7:25	8:22	9:05
Scarsdale	7:42	-	9:22
Bronxville	8:05	-	9:40
Harlem 125th St.	8:24	-	9:59
Grand Central Terminal	8:30	8:59	10:06

I live in White Plains. I need a train that will arrive in New York City around 9:00 a.m. Could I take the 8:22 express?

1. *Yes, you could take the 8:22* ______________.

I live in White Plains. I'm meeting my boss at Grand Central Station at 8:45 a.m. We're going to an important meeting and I can't be late. Which train should I take?

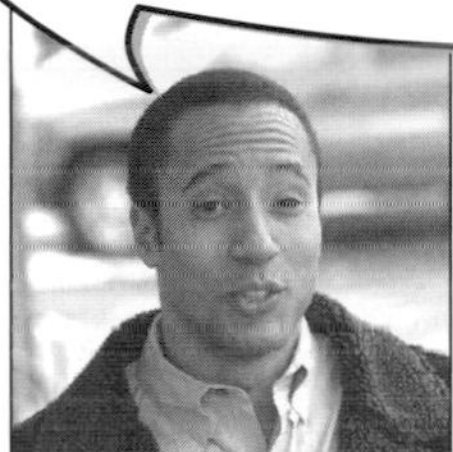

2. ______________________________.

I live in Scarsdale. I've got some free time tomorrow morning. I need to go shopping for a new laptop in New York City. Most computer stores open at 10:00 a.m. What time should I be at the Scarsdale train station?

3. ______________________________.

I'm in White Plains. I want to go to Bronxville. Could I take an express train or should I take a local?

4. ______________________________.

LESSON 2

 **Complete the conversation. Use words from the box.**

limousine	going	should	late	arriving	reservation	rental

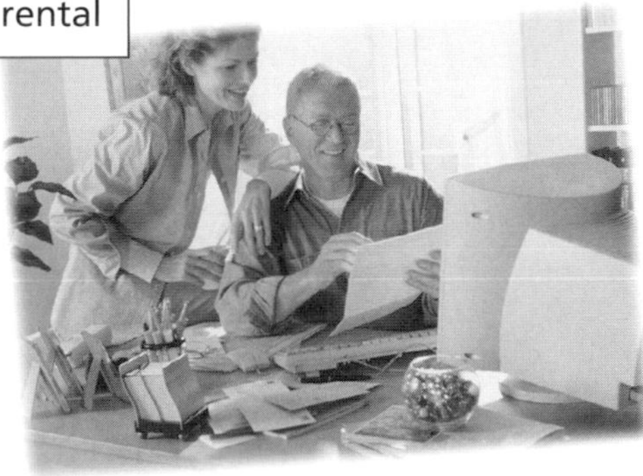

A: What time are we ________ (1.) in Copenhagen?

B: Pretty ________ (2.). Around 10:30 p.m.

A: What about a hotel?

B: I'm going to make a ________ (3.) online.

A: Great. And are we ________ (4.) to need a taxi to the hotel?

B: There's a ________ (5.) from the airport, or we could get a ________ (6.) car.

A: They're expensive. I think we ________ (7.) save our money.

B: You're right. And walking is good exercise.

9 **What are they going to do? Write the letter on the line.**

1. ____ She's going to make a reservation.
2. ____ He's going to get in at 8:45.
3. ____ She's going to take a limo.
4. ____ He's not going to take a taxi.

10 **Read the responses. Complete each question with <u>be going to</u> and the base form of the verb.**

1. **A:** Where *is Paul going to meet us* ____________________?
   B: Paul's going to meet us at the airport café.
2. **A:** Who ____________________?
   B: I think Gretchen is going to buy the tickets.
3. **A:** When ____________________?
   B: I'm going to need the rental car on Thursday and Friday.
4. **A:** What time ____________________?
   B: They're going to arrive at 5:50 p.m.
5. **A:** ____________________ our 6:20 flight?
   B: Yes, we'll make it.

The world's longest direct run train (without changing trains) is 10,214 km, from Moscow, Russia, to Pyongyang, North Korea. One train a week takes this route. The trip takes almost eight days!

Source: www.guinnessworldrecords.com

11 WHAT ABOUT YOU? **What are your plans for today? Complete the chart. Put a check ✓ in the box.**

	I did this.	I'm going to do this.	I'm not going to do this.
call a friend			
check my e-mail			
go shopping			
clean my house			
cook			
study			
exercise			
take a taxi			
other . . .			

12 **Now write sentences about your plans for today. Use the future tense with be going to.**

I'm going to call a friend tonight after work.

LESSONS 3 AND 4

13 **Who is speaking? Write a gate agent or a passenger on the line.**

Good afternoon, ladies and gentlemen. Flight 58 has been delayed. The new departure time is 7:00.

1. *a gate agent*

We got bumped from our flight. What should we do?

2. ______________________

We are now boarding first class passengers for Asiana Flight 58. Please have your boarding passes ready.

3. ______________________

a gate agent

a passenger

The flight is overbooked. I think I'm going to volunteer to take a later flight.

4. ______________________

Can I still make the 6:45 flight to São Paulo?

5. ______________________

This is a gate change for Asiana Airlines, Flight 58, with service to Tokyo, Japan. The new gate is Gate 8G.

6. ______________________

Look at the pictures. Match each statement with the correct picture.

1. ____ Our flight was canceled. The airplane had mechanical problems.
2. ____ The cruise was terrible. My whole family got seasick!
3. ____ Sorry we're late. We missed the express train and had to take a local.
4. ____ My dad had to wait over an hour to get through security.
5. ____ We had an accident. Our sightseeing bus hit a tree.

15 **Look at the pictures of Joe Cooney's trip. Then read the statements.**
Check ✓ true or false.

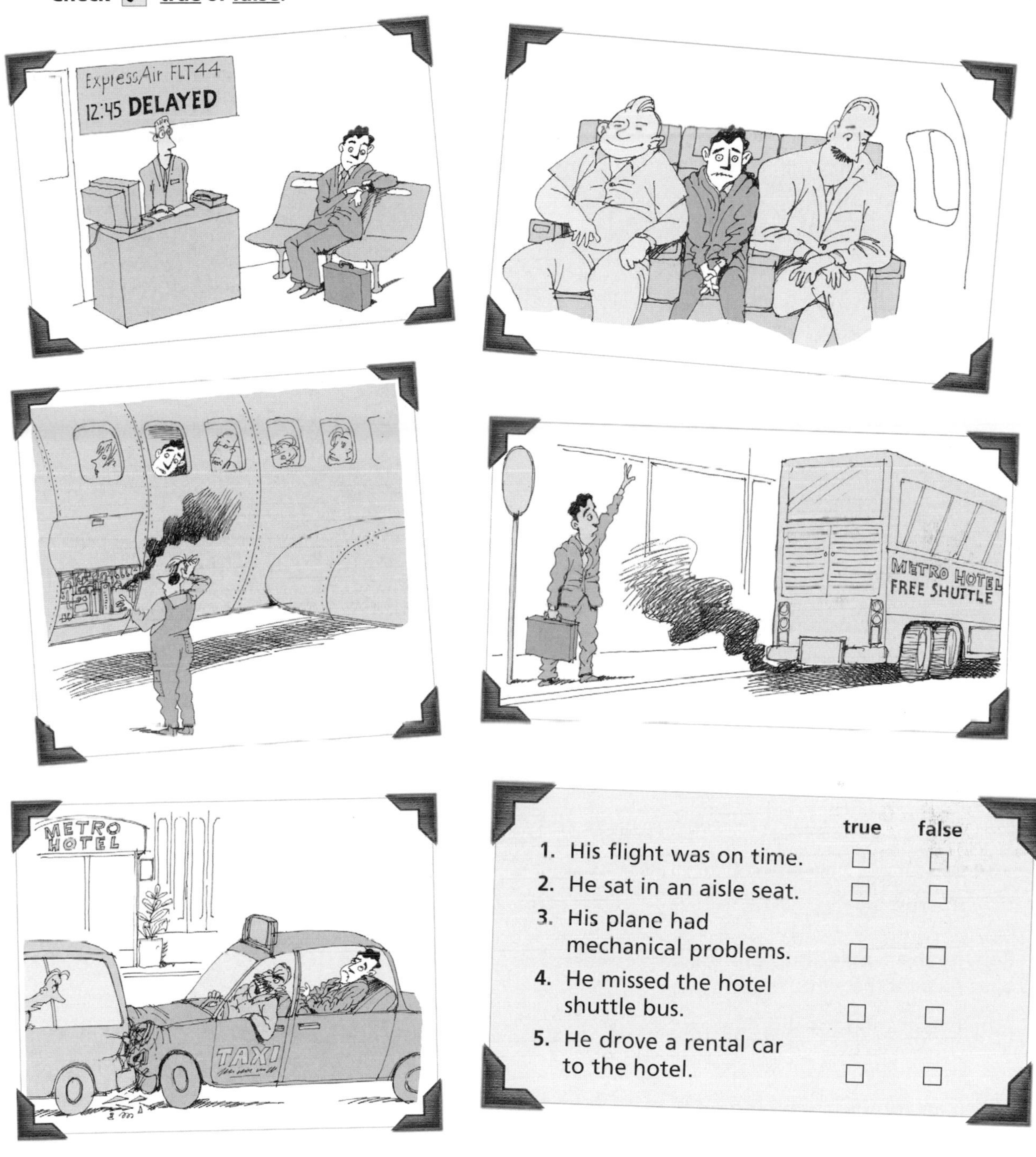

	true	false
1. His flight was on time.	☐	☐
2. He sat in an aisle seat.	☐	☐
3. His plane had mechanical problems.	☐	☐
4. He missed the hotel shuttle bus.	☐	☐
5. He drove a rental car to the hotel.	☐	☐

16 **Write a short paragraph about Joe Cooney's trip.**

GRAMMAR BOOSTER

A **Read the questions and statements. Correct the mistakes.**

1. You should ~~to go~~ go to track 57.
2. Where could he to get a train to Hampstead?
3. Bette can't takes a flight to Tokyo.
4. When we could leave?
5. How late can he to board?
6. He shoulds choose an aisle seat.

B **Read the questions. Complete the responses.**

1. **A:** Should she buy a one-way ticket?
   B: No, she shouldn't. It's more expensive.
2. **A:** Can he bring food on the flight?
   B: Yes, ______________________.
3. **A:** Could I take the number 3 train?
   B: Yes, ______________________. It will take you to the right station.
4. **A:** Can we get seats together?
   B: No, ______________________. I'm sorry. We only have a few seats left.
5. **A:** Should they get a rental car?
   B: Yes, ______________________. It is more convenient.

C **Rewrite the sentences to express future actions. Use <u>be going to</u> and the base form of the verb.**

1. She studied for three hours.
   She's going to study for three hours tomorrow.
2. They ran two miles last Sunday.
   ______________________________________ next Sunday.
3. We had a party last week.
   ______________________________________ next week.
4. I went to school yesterday.
   ______________________________________ tomorrow.
5. You did a great job.
   ______________________________________.

JUST FOR **FUN**

Look at the sentences. Write the words. Then look at the gray boxes ▢.

1. The plane is full. I'm going to ____ to be bumped.
2. We were late because the plane had mechanical ____.
3. The agent at the gate needs to see your ____ pass.
4. I'm going to have to cancel my hotel ____.
5. We should hurry. There's always a line at the ____ gate.
6. I don't have to take the early train, but I ____.

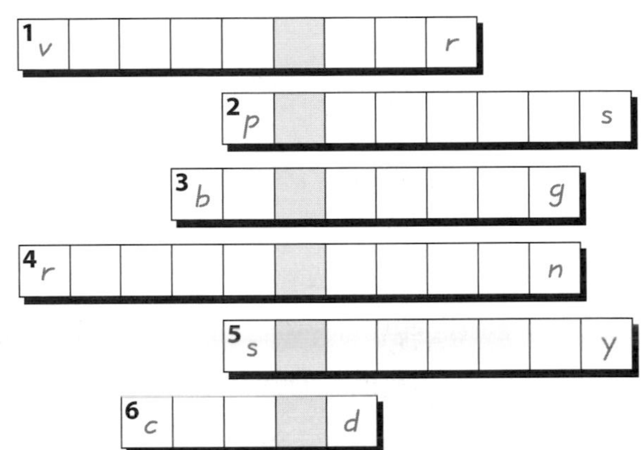

What's the new word? ______________

Read the poem. Can you solve the riddle?

As I was going to St. Ives

by Mother Goose*

As I was going to St. Ives,
I met a man with seven wives;
Every wife had seven sacks,
Every sack had seven cats,
Every cat had seven kits;
Kits, cats, sacks, and wives,
How many were going to St. Ives?

*"Mother Goose" rhymes are traditional English poems for children. No one knows who wrote them.

Answer: One.

UNIT 10

Shopping Smart

TOPIC PREVIEW

1 **How do you use an ATM machine? Look at the pictures on the left. Match each picture with an instruction on the right.**

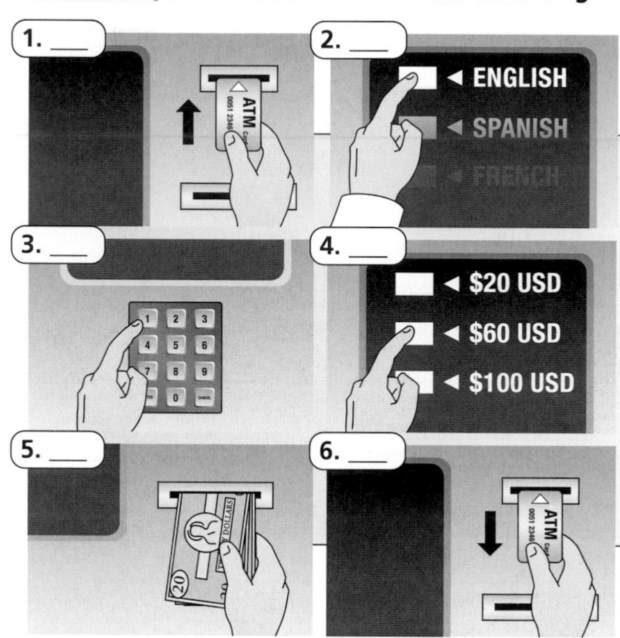

a. Take your ATM card.
b. Enter the amount of cash you want.
c. Take your cash.
d. Put your ATM card in the card slot.
e. Choose your language.
f. Enter your Personal Identification Number (PIN).

2 WHAT ABOUT YOU? **Look at the list on the left. In your <u>own</u> country, what could people use to pay for these things? Check ✓ the boxes.**

	Cash	Credit Card	Traveler's Check
dinner at a restaurant	❒	❒	❒
a newspaper from a newsstand	❒	❒	❒
an airplane ticket	❒	❒	❒
a CD from an online music store	❒	❒	❒
a snack in a convenience store	❒	❒	❒
a hotel room	❒	❒	❒

LESSON 1

3 **Choose the correct response. Circle the letter.**

1. "I'm looking for an MP3 player for my son."
   a. You think so? b. What about this one? c. It's the best.
2. "How much did you want to spend?"
   a. I wanted $100. b. No more than $100. c. I spent $100.
3. "We have two or three in your price range."
   a. It can't hurt to ask. b. Could I have a look? c. Good idea.
4. "Why do you recommend Diego brand DVD players?"
   a. They're the easiest to use. b. They're the least popular. c. They're the worst.

4 **Complete the conversation. Write the letter on the line.**

A: Excuse me. I'd like to buy a camcorder.
B: ______ 1.
A: I don't know. What do you recommend?
B: ______ 2.
A: Actually, that's a little out of my price range.
B: ______ 3.
A: Is it difficult to use?
B: ______ 4.
A: OK. Do you accept traveler's checks?
B: ______ 5.

a. The Power X. It's the most popular.
b. No. And the sound is great.
c. OK. Which one are you interested in?
d. Yes. No problem.
e. The X23 isn't bad, and it's much cheaper.

5 **Look at the chart from a digital camera buying guide.**

COMPARE DIGITAL CAMERAS

Brand / Model	Price	Ease of Use	Size	Weight
 Diego Mini 3000	US$239	●●	c	35 g (1.2 oz)
 Honshu B100	US$209	●●●	p	283 g (9.9 oz)
 Honshu X24	US$139	●	s	180 g (6.3 oz)
 Prego 5	US$299	●●●●	s	135 g (4.7 oz)
 Vision 2.0	US$449	●●●	s	224 g (7.9 oz)

KEY

●●●●	very easy
●●●	pretty easy
●●	a little difficult
●	difficult
c	compact (small size, can fit in a shirt pocket)
s	standard (medium size, similar to a point and shoot camera)
p	professional (large size, similar to a 35mm camera)

Now write questions with Which. Use the superlative form of the adjectives from the box. Not all adjectives will be used.

~~expensive~~	light	portable	easy to use	cheap	heavy	difficult to use

1. A: *Which camera is the most expensive*?
   B: The Vision 2.0.
2. A: ______________________?
   B: The Honshu X24.
3. A: ______________________?
   B: The Diego Mini 3000.
4. A: ______________________?
   B: The Prego 5.
5. A: ______________________?
   B: The Honshu B100.

 **Read each person's statements. For each shopper, recommend a digital camera from the buying guide in Exercise 5. Give a reason for your advice.**

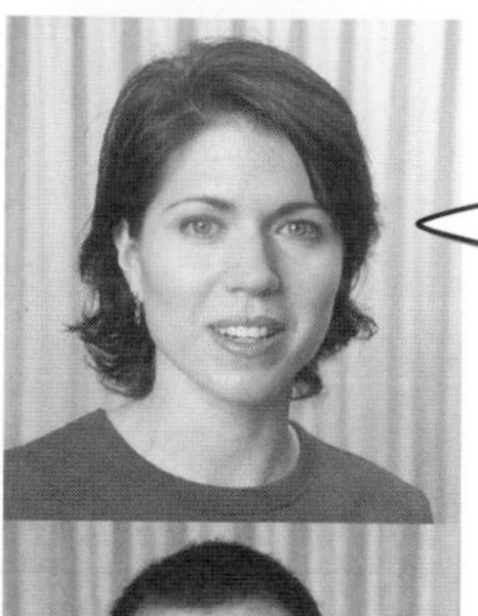

"I need a new camera. The one I have now is too heavy. I really want a camera that I can carry in my jacket pocket."

1.  ______________________.

"I'm looking for a digital camera for my mother. She isn't good with electronics, so it must be very easy to use. What do you recommend?"

2.  ______________________.

"I'd like to have a look at your least expensive digital camera. I can't spend more than $150. Do you have anything in my price range?"

3. YOU ______________________.

LESSON 2

 **Complete the conversations. Use words from the box.**

give	fair	too	much
about	more	bowl	enough

A: This ________ (1.) is gorgeous. I'd love to get it for my sister.

B: It's nice. And it's small ________ (2.) to take in your suitcase.

A: I'm going to ask about the price. I hope it's not ________ (3.) expensive.

A: I'm interested in this bowl. How ________ (4.) do you want for it?

C: This one is $45.

A: That's a bit ________ (5.) than I want to spend. I could ________ (6.) you $30.

C: How ________ (7.) $35? That's a bargain.

A: OK. That sounds ________ (8.).

The largest shopping center in the world is West Edmonton Mall, in Edmonton, Alberta, Canada. The mall covers 493,000 sq. meters (5.3 million square feet), and has over 800 stores and services.

The mall complex includes the world's largest indoor amusement park and the world's largest indoor lake. More than 23,000 people work there. And the mall has one more superlative—the world's largest parking lot!

What's the largest shopping center in your city or town?

____

Source: www.westedmall.com

8 **Complete the sentences. Use too or enough and the adjective in parentheses.**

1. I'm not going to read that book. It's ____________________ (boring).
2. Sylvia shouldn't travel alone. She isn't ____________________ (old).
3. I don't want to buy anything in that shop. The people were ____________________ (unfriendly).
4. Tania likes the red rug, but it's ____________________ (big) for her living room.
5. I love this belt, but it isn't ____________________ (long). I need a size 34.
6. Are your shoes ____________________ (comfortable)? We're going to do a lot of walking.
7. We wanted to bargain for a lower price, but it was ____________________ (difficult).

LESSONS 3 AND 4

9 **Choose the correct response. Write the response on the line.**

You think so? / What a rip-off! / Thanks. Keep the change. / What a good deal! / The tall one?

1. A: $650! I paid $329 for the same camcorder yesterday!
   B: ______________________________
2. A: How much do you want for this vase?
   B: ______________________________
3. A: You could try to get a better price.
   B: ______________________________
4. A: I saved a lot of money on this DVD player. It was only $79.
   B: ______________________________
5. A: Here you are, sir. The Atlas Hotel. That's $8.50.
   B: ______________________________

10 **Read the statements and questions. Who would probably say this?**
Check ✔ the boxes.

	Buyer	Seller
1. "All of our scanners are on sale."	❐	❐
2. "I'm almost out of cash."	❐	❐
3. "That's out of my price range."	❐	❐
4. "Wow! What a great deal!"	❐	❐
5. "How about this one? It's our most popular brand."	❐	❐
6. "Can you give me a better price?"	❐	❐

11 **Read the article about bargaining customs around the world. Then read the statements. Check ✓ true or false.**

Can you give me a better price?

Bargaining Customs Around the World

Bargaining customs are very different around the world. Few tourists would go shopping in another country without knowing the exchange rate. However, many travelers don't learn anything about the local shopping customs of the place they are visiting before spending money. Understanding when it's OK to bargain can save you a lot of money and make your shopping experience much more enjoyable.

In some countries, bargaining is an important part of the shopping culture. In others, bargaining is not done at all. Here's a bargaining guide for some countries around the world:

Morocco: Bargaining is always expected in the shopping markets. Here bargaining is more than just getting the best price. If you go into a shop and agree to the first price a seller offers, the seller may not be happy. For Moroccans, bargaining is a form of entertainment; it's a game of skill, a little bit of acting, and it's a chance to chat about the weather, business, and family. So be sure to have fun and try to get a better price!

Switzerland: Bargaining is not the custom here. Shop clerks can almost never give you a lower price. However, some hotels may give you a lower rate during the less popular times of year. It can't hurt to ask.

Tahiti: Bargaining is not appropriate in the South Pacific. In fact, it is considered disrespectful to ask for a better price. In the food markets, sellers will even take their fruits and vegetables back home with them, rather than give a discount!

SOURCE: "Lonely Planet Travel Guides"

	true	false
1. Bargaining customs are similar around the world.	☐	☐
2. Generally, market sellers in Morocco love to bargain.	☐	☐
3. In Switzerland, it's OK to bargain for a cheaper hotel room.	☐	☐
4. It can't hurt to ask a fruit seller in Tahiti for a lower price.	☐	☐

12 WHAT ABOUT YOU? **Write a short paragraph about bargaining in your own country. What items do people bargain for? What items do people never bargain for?**

GRAMMAR BOOSTER

A **Complete the chart.**

	Adjective	Comparative form	Superlative form
1.	beautiful		
2.			the most intelligent
3.	big		
4.		more convenient	
5.	busy		
6.			the fastest
7.		safer	
8.	noisy		

B **Complete the conversations with the comparative or the superlative form of the adjective in parentheses.**

1. **A:** Which one of these three sweaters do you think is _the prettiest_ (pretty)?
   B: The blue one. The other two are not attractive at all.
2. **A:** How do you like the book?
   B: I don't like it. It's __________ (bad) than the one I read yesterday.
3. **A:** Did you enjoy Australia?
   B: Yes. I think it's one of __________ (interesting) places in the world.
4. **A:** Who is __________ (good) at baseball, you or your brother?
   B: Well, I'm a __________ (fast) base runner, but my brother is a __________ (powerful) hitter. Actually, my dad is the __________ (good) player in the family. He was a star player in college.
5. **A:** Which laptop is __________ (popular)?
   B: Well, the X102 is the __________ (cheap) model in the store. But I actually recommend the X200. It's a little __________ (expensive) than the X102, but much __________ (light).

C **Answer the questions. Use <u>too</u> or <u>enough</u> and the adjective in parentheses.**

1. **A:** Why didn't you buy the camcorder?
   B: (expensive) _It was too expensive_. I need to save money this month.
2. **A:** Is the food too spicy?
   B: (spicy) ____________________. I'm going to ask for more hot sauce!
3. **A:** What's wrong with these shoes?
   B: I can't wear them. (uncomfortable) ____________________.
4. **A:** Why don't you like the apartment?
   B: (noisy) ____________________. I'm looking for a quiet neighborhood.
5. **A:** Why don't you take the train instead of flying?
   B: (fast) ____________________. I have to get there as soon as possible.
6. **A:** Do you want to go to a jazz concert?
   B: Thanks for asking, but I'm not a jazz music fan. (boring) ____________________.

JUST FOR **FUN**

 **Complete the crossword puzzle.**

Across

1. opposite of best
2. opposite of most
3. the amount something costs
4. ask for a better price

Down

5. pay money
6. a low price; a great ___
7. money you give a waiter or driver
8. money you can pay; your price ___
9. help you get in a restaurant or hotel

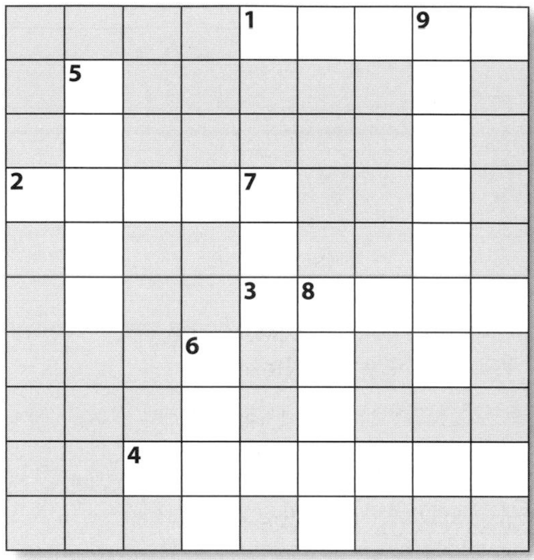

 **Which words go together? Circle the adjectives with <u>opposite</u> meanings.**

1. old	healthy	big	new
2. comfortable	large	sweet	small
3. gorgeous	difficult	easy	loose
4. interesting	pretty	fatty	boring
5. expensive	hot	cheap	wild
6. different	similar	nice	formal
7. light	flattering	heavy	unusual
8. liberal	short	portable	long
9. conservative	popular	good	bad